D0497563

Lawson, Jane, 1968–
Tossed : 200 fast,
fresh, and fabulous sala
2005.
33305209455405
la   05/16/06

tossed

200 fast, fresh, and fabulous salads

Jane Lawson

Photography by Tim Robinson
Styling by Sarah DeNardi

THUNDER BAY
P · R · E · S · S

San Diego, California

Thunder Bay Press
An imprint of the Advantage Publishers Group
5880 Oberlin Drive, San Diego, CA 92121–4794
www.thunderbaybooks.com

Text, design, photography, and illustrations © Murdoch Books Pty Limited, 2005.

Copyright under International, Pan American, and Universal Copyright Conventions. All rights reserved. No part of this publication may be reproduced or transmitted in any form or by any means, electronic or mechanical, including photocopying, recording, or by any information storage-and-retrieval system, without written permission from the copyright holder. Brief passages (not to exceed 1,000 words) may be quoted for reviews.

All notations of errors or omissions should be addressed to Thunder Bay Press, Editorial Department, at the above address. All other correspondence (author inquiries, permissions, and rights) concerning the content of this book should be addressed to Murdoch Books, Pier 8/9, 23 Hickson Road, Millers Point NSW 2000, Australia.

NOTE: Those who might be at risk from the effects of salmonella poisoning (the elderly, pregnant women, young children, and those with a compromised immune system) should consult their physician before trying recipes with raw eggs.

ISBN 1-59223-418-6
Library of Congress Cataloging-in-Publication Data available upon request

Printed in China by Midas Printing (Asia) Ltd.
1 2 3 4 5 09 08 07 06 05

Concept and art direction: Marylouise Brammer
Photographer: Tim Robinson
Stylist: Sarah DeNardi
Recipes by: Murdoch Books Test Kitchen
Recipe introductions by: Francesca Newby
Editors: Grace Cheetham, Katri Hilden
Designer: Annette Fitzgerald
Production: Monika Vidovic
Stylist's assistants: Julie Ray, Loren Trompp

The publisher and stylist would like to thank the following companies for generously loaning furniture, fabric, and tableware for photography: ECC Lighting and Living, Great Dane, Orrefors Kosta Boda, Georg Jensen, Royal Copenhagen, Tsunami, Villeroy & Boch, Waterford Wedgwood. Special thanks also go to the following companies: Chee Soon & Fitzgerald for their fantastic Marimekko fabrics; Design Mode International for their iittala tableware; Dinosaur Designs; Foxes for the models' clothing; Bisanna and Marble Works for tiles; Mokum Textiles for their Osborne & Little and Liberty fabrics and wallpapers; Mud; Paper Couture for their gorgeous paper lunch boxes; and Signature Prints for their Florence Broadhurst fabrics and wallpapers. Finally a heartfelt thanks to our patient models Loren, Felix, Max, Ava, and Ruby and wonderful assistants Loren and Julie.

Lawson, Jane, 1968–
Tossed : 200 fast,
fresh, and fabulous sala
2005.
33305209455405
la   05/16/06

tossed

200 fast, fresh, and fabulous salads

Jane Lawson

Photography by Tim Robinson
Styling by Sarah DeNardi

THUNDER BAY
P · R · E · S · S

San Diego, California

Thunder Bay Press
An imprint of the Advantage Publishers Group
5880 Oberlin Drive, San Diego, CA 92121–4794
www.thunderbaybooks.com

Text, design, photography, and illustrations © Murdoch Books Pty Limited, 2005.

Copyright under International, Pan American, and Universal Copyright Conventions. All rights reserved. No part of this publication may be reproduced or transmitted in any form or by any means, electronic or mechanical, including photocopying, recording, or by any information storage-and-retrieval system, without written permission from the copyright holder. Brief passages (not to exceed 1,000 words) may be quoted for reviews.

All notations of errors or omissions should be addressed to Thunder Bay Press, Editorial Department, at the above address. All other correspondence (author inquiries, permissions, and rights) concerning the content of this book should be addressed to Murdoch Books, Pier 8/9, 23 Hickson Road, Millers Point NSW 2000, Australia.

NOTE: Those who might be at risk from the effects of salmonella poisoning (the elderly, pregnant women, young children, and those with a compromised immune system) should consult their physician before trying recipes with raw eggs.

ISBN 1-59223-418-6
Library of Congress Cataloging-in-Publication Data available upon request

Printed in China by Midas Printing (Asia) Ltd.
1 2 3 4 5 09 08 07 06 05

Concept and art direction: Marylouise Brammer
Photographer: Tim Robinson
Stylist: Sarah DeNardi
Recipes by: Murdoch Books Test Kitchen
Recipe introductions by: Francesca Newby
Editors: Grace Cheetham, Katri Hilden
Designer: Annette Fitzgerald
Production: Monika Vidovic
Stylist's assistants: Julie Ray, Loren Trompp

The publisher and stylist would like to thank the following companies for generously loaning furniture, fabric, and tableware for photography: ECC Lighting and Living, Great Dane, Orrefors Kosta Boda, Georg Jensen, Royal Copenhagen, Tsunami, Villeroy & Boch, Waterford Wedgwood. Special thanks also go to the following companies: Chee Soon & Fitzgerald for their fantastic Marimekko fabrics; Design Mode International for their iittala tableware; Dinosaur Designs; Foxes for the models' clothing; Bisanna and Marble Works for tiles; Mokum Textiles for their Osborne & Little and Liberty fabrics and wallpapers; Mud; Paper Couture for their gorgeous paper lunch boxes; and Signature Prints for their Florence Broadhurst fabrics and wallpapers. Finally a heartfelt thanks to our patient models Loren, Felix, Max, Ava, and Ruby and wonderful assistants Loren and Julie.

contents

toss it   For far too long, salads have been relegated to the side of the plate. It's time these life-giving, energy-boosting meals were treated with a little respect. A mighty source of nutrients, a gift of

nature's bounty, salads are blessed with virtues too numerous to list. For hot days, cold days, lunch with the gals, or lunch on the run, nothing beats a salad, so look to your crisper and get tossing!

toss it

There is no better showcase for truly fresh produce than a salad, be it ripe tomatoes bursting with flavor, succulent shrimp rich with the taste of the ocean, or crumbly, creamy feta with its salty tang. The joy of a great salad lies in celebrating all the pleasures of authentic ingredients in peak condition.

The versatility of salad is one of its greatest assets. When you need a simple meal that can be thrown together in an instant, a fresh, leafy ensemble full of crisp raw vegetables dressed with a classic vinaigrette is just the first option. There are infinite recipes for absolutely gorgeous salads that involve little more effort than some chopping and tossing, yet don't compromise on taste.

Sometimes, though, there's nothing quite so satisfying as rolling up your sleeves, taking over the kitchen, and creating a complex, intricate meal offering sophisticated new flavors. Again, there is a salad to suit. Experimentation is one of the great joys of cooking, and salads offer enormous scope for innovation and discovery. Whatever taste you are seeking out, creating a dish with a real depth of flavor, or which somehow tastes fresh and new, is its own reward. For example, there are wonderfully intense Asian dressings that require dozens of ingredients, four different steps, and a good half hour to prepare. The deeper pleasure of taking the time to create something rare and special, especially when you're cooking for others, is an experience just begging to be shared.

There is, of course, more to salad than sheer good taste. The benefits of eating fresh vegetables are so widely acknowledged that it would be redundant to point them out again. However, we sometimes forget the value of eating a wide variety of different foods. To satisfy your body's need for the full range of vitamins and minerals, eating vegetables alone is simply not enough. We also need to find a way to include nuts, dairy, meat, seafood, fruit, seeds, beans, and grains in our diet, both in the right balance and on a regular basis. Again, here is where the humble salad comes into its own, gathering an abundance of health-giving ingredients in ways that are limited only by your taste and your imagination. A rainbow of vegetables, slivers of salty ham, shavings of Parmesan cheese, a handful of nuts, and a heap of leafy greens in one meal is more than just a good start. And eating a variety of salads throughout the week is a delicious way of ensuring you meet all your dietary needs.

Of course, salads are also a dieter's best friend. Few of us have the discipline or willpower to be sensible all of the time. The weekend blowout is a common feature of life, whether it's the slice of cake you swore you wouldn't have, or maybe those two extra glasses of wine you definitely shouldn't have had! So if you can't be good all of the time, the next best option is to be really good most of the time. Luckily, piling up on salad during the week is an excellent way to make sure those weekend lapses don't ruin all your hard work.

Presentation is an aspect of food that is all too often just an afterthought, yet when we eat, as with all the pleasures of the body, we are engaging all our senses. Taste and smell are obviously dominant, but there is an extra element of delight involved in eating a meal that looks superb. Happily, there is something innately appealing about a mound of fresh, colorful food glistening under a light coating of dressing.

The way you choose to serve the meal is as important as the way you dress the table. While white plates are a definite classic, there is no need to limit yourself—don't be afraid to use color on the table, especially when serving a salad. The jewel hues of raw vegetables, the soft creamy tones of cheese, and the smoky notes of roasted vegetables are all enhanced by a blast of color on the table.

Many salads look wonderful heaped high on communal platters, and there's always something invitingly intimate about serving each other at the table. Other salads are better suited to individual plates and bowls, since the construction of the meal is part of its charm. However you choose to serve the meal, give free rein to your imagination when it comes to styling the table. Quirky accessories, sensuous fabrics, and arresting colors can only enhance the pleasure of eating.

The key to it all is to keep the basics simple, then dress it up with your own individual touches that reflect your personal style. Seasonal food, fresh flavors, and a burst of life-affirming color are all you really need to create a memorable meal.

poolside Lounging around the pool or by the barbecue on a sparkling sunny day calls for an atmosphere of effortless luxury. When it comes to food, super-fresh, top-quality ingredients simply

prepared and beautifully presented are all you need to make a splash. A sizzling grill and a table laden with big bowls of salad set the scene for a perfect feast in the sun.

There is no better place to soak up the long days of summer than by the pool. Big umbrellas, chaise longues, and a long, cool drink are some essential props and accessories that will create the right mood, but it's the food that sits at the heart of any event. Simple, light, and fresh are the key qualities of summer eating, and nothing quite fits the bill like a sensational selection of salads. Nobody wants to fill up when they're frolicking by the water. It's not just about looking good in your swimwear but about feeling satiated, yet still light and active. Salads are the ultimate in lightweight cuisine, and you can pack a heap of super flavors into a salad without a sense of having gone over the top, or you can keep it simple by going for a leafy base topped with one or two intense additions. Either way, you've got the perfect combination for a party by the pool. Stylish entertaining without the stress is the mantra of poolside dining, and salads are the perfect way to achieve that balance between easy and elegant. Keeping it casual means you can relax and join in the fun, but there's no point in entertaining if you forget to make it special. Luckily, it's so simple to achieve a feeling of plenty—just lay out a spread of delectable dishes and break open a loaf of crispy, crusty bread. When dishing up poolside, take your cue from the elements and go for a simple, effortless look that reflects the myriad blues of the water and sky, stylishly accented with notes of crisp white. Cool patterns and unusual accessories help bring an eclectic modern edge to a timeless setting.

seared tuna, penne, and green bean salad

2 cups green beans, trimmed and cut into short lengths
4 cups penne rigate
9 oz. fresh tuna steak

1/2 cup olive oil
1 red onion, thinly sliced
1 tablespoon balsamic vinegar

Boil, steam, or microwave the beans until tender but still crisp. Drain, refresh under cold water, then drain again and transfer to a serving bowl.

Cook the pasta in a large pot of boiling salted water until al dente. Drain, refresh under cold water, and drain again. Add to the beans.

Meanwhile, preheat the grill or a charbroil pan to medium. Brush the tuna with a little of the oil and cook on the grill until seared on the outside and still pink inside—about 3–4 minutes on each side. Remove from the heat, allow to stand for 2–3 minutes, and cut into thick slices.

Heat half the oil in a frying pan. Add the onion and gently sauté until softened, about 5–6 minutes. Add the vinegar, turn the heat up high, and quickly cook until the dressing has reduced. Add the onion mixture to the pasta with the tuna and remaining oil, then lightly toss together with some salt and pepper to taste. Cool to room temperature before serving.

Serves 4

penne with shrimp

3 plum tomatoes
5 cups penne
1 lb. raw shrimp, peeled and
    deveined, tails intact
1 tablespoon olive oil
2 cups baby spinach leaves
4 1/2 oz. goat cheese, crumbled
1/4 cup pine nuts, toasted

lemon and garlic dressing
2 garlic cloves, crushed
3 tablespoons extra-virgin
    olive oil
2 teaspoons finely grated
    lemon zest
2 tablespoons lemon juice
1 tablespoon chopped Italian
    parsley

Preheat the oven to 350°F. Cut each tomato into six wedges and bake for 45 minutes or until they are just starting to dry out around the edges. Remove and cool. Meanwhile, cook the penne in a large pot of boiling salted water until al dente. Drain well, allow to cool, and transfer to a large bowl.

Preheat the grill or a charbroil pan to high. Toss the shrimp in the oil and cook until just opaque, about 2–3 minutes. Mix into the pasta with the tomato, spinach, and goat cheese. Combine the dressing ingredients and gently toss through. Sprinkle with pine nuts and serve.

Serves 4

Slippery, slithery noodles hide a host of plump, sweet shrimp in this crisp and nutty, light and lively salad.

shrimp and rice noodle salad

9 oz. rice stick noodles
1 1/2 lb. raw shrimp, peeled and
  deveined, tails intact
1 tablespoon olive oil
1 carrot, finely julienned
1 cucumber, seeded and
  julienned
2 large handfuls cilantro leaves
1/2 cup roasted unsalted
  peanuts, chopped
1/3 cup crisp fried shallots
  (see Note)

dressing
1/2 cup rice vinegar
1 tablespoon brown sugar
1 garlic clove, finely chopped
2 red chilies, finely chopped
3 tablespoons fish sauce
3 tablespoons lime juice
2 tablespoons peanut oil

Put the noodles in a large heatproof bowl, cover with boiling water, and allow to soak for 10 minutes. Drain, rinse under cold water to cool, then drain again. Place in a large serving bowl.

Meanwhile, preheat the grill or a charbroil pan to high. Toss the shrimp in the oil and cook until just opaque, about 2–3 minutes. Take the shrimp off the heat and mix them into the noodles with the carrot, cucumber, and cilantro.

To make the dressing, combine the vinegar, sugar, and garlic in a small saucepan. Bring to a boil, then reduce the heat and simmer for 3 minutes to reduce slightly. Pour into a bowl and add the chili, fish sauce, and lime juice. Slowly whisk in the oil, and season to taste.

Toss the dressing through the salad, sprinkle with the peanuts and crisp fried shallots, and serve.

Note: Crisp fried shallots are red Asian shallot flakes used as a garnish in Southeast Asia. They are available from Asian markets.

Serves 4

shrimp and rice noodle salad

charbroiled polenta with shaved fennel salad

2 cups milk
1¼ cups polenta (cornmeal)
    (don't use instant polenta)
⅓ cup grated Parmesan
    cheese, plus 1 cup shaved
    Parmesan cheese

1 tablespoon butter
2 baby fennel bulbs, trimmed
    (reserve the fronds)
1⅓ cups watercress leaves
1 tablespoon lemon juice
1½ tablespoons olive oil

Bring the milk and 2 cups water to a boil in a heavy-based saucepan. Add the polenta in a thin, steady stream and whisk thoroughly. Reduce the heat as low as possible and simmer for 30–40 minutes, stirring occasionally. Remove from the heat, stir in the grated Parmesan and butter, and season well. Pour into an oiled square dish and set aside for 30 minutes to cool and set. When cooled, cut into four squares, then cut each square diagonally to yield eight triangles. Brush with a little oil and cook in a hot charbroil pan until brown grill marks appear.

Slice the fennel very thinly and chop the fronds. Toss in a bowl with the watercress, lemon juice, oil, and half the shaved Parmesan. Season well. Stack two polenta triangles on each serving plate, pile the salad on top, sprinkle with the remaining shaved Parmesan, and serve.

Serves 4

steamed corn salad with Asian dressing

1 large red bell pepper
3 corncobs, husks and silks
    removed
1 cup bean sprouts, trimmed
4 scallions, thinly sliced
    diagonally

Asian dressing
1/2 teaspoon crushed garlic
1/2 teaspoon finely grated
    fresh ginger
1 teaspoon sugar
1 tablespoon rice vinegar
1 tablespoon soy sauce
1 tablespoon lemon juice
2 teaspoons sesame oil
2 tablespoons peanut oil

Cut the bell pepper into large flat pieces and remove the seeds and membranes. Cook, skin side up, under a hot broiler until the skin blackens and blisters. Cool in a plastic bag, then peel away the skin and cut the flesh into large strips.

Slice each corncob into six rounds. Steam for 5–8 minutes or until tender. Arrange on a serving plate with the bell pepper and bean sprouts.

Whisk all the Asian dressing ingredients together in a small bowl and season with pepper. Drizzle over the salad, sprinkle with the scallions, and serve.

Serves 4 as a side salad

Fresh tuna brings a tender touch to this contemporary version of a timeless French classic.

modern salad Niçoise

3 tablespoons lemon juice
1 garlic clove, crushed
2/3 cup olive oil
3 waxy potatoes, such
    as fingerling
3 eggs
1 cup green beans, trimmed
1 green bell pepper, sliced
heaping 3/4 cup black olives

3 firm ripe tomatoes, cut into
    wedges
1/2 cucumber, cut into chunks
3 scallions, cut into 3/4-inch
    lengths
1 1/4 lb. fresh tuna steaks

Put the lemon juice, garlic, and 1/2 cup of the oil in a screw-top jar, season well, and shake vigorously to combine.

Cook the potatoes in a pot of boiling salted water for 10–12 minutes or until tender, adding the eggs for the final 8 minutes of cooking. Drain.

Cool the eggs under cold water, then peel and quarter them. Allow the potatoes to cool, then cut into chunks and place in a large bowl.

Bring another pot of lightly salted water to a boil, add the beans, and blanch for 3 minutes or until just tender. Drain and refresh under cold water. Drain again, then slice diagonally and add to the potato with the bell pepper, olives, tomatoes, cucumber, and scallions.

Strain the garlic from the dressing, then shake again to combine. Pour half over the salad, toss through gently, and transfer to a serving dish.

Meanwhile, preheat the grill or a charbroil pan to medium. Brush the tuna with the remaining oil and season well on both sides. Cook until seared on the outside and still pink inside—about 3–4 minutes on each side. Remove from the heat, allow to cool for 5 minutes, then slice thinly. Arrange on top of the salad with the egg quarters, drizzle with the remaining dressing, and serve.

Serves 4

charbroiled polenta with shaved fennel salad

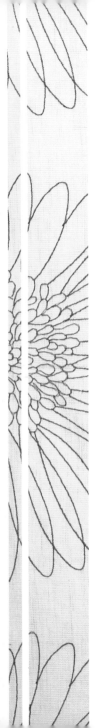

goat cheese, avocado, and smoked salmon salad

2 tablespoons extra-virgin
   olive oil
1 tablespoon balsamic vinegar
1 avocado
1 cup baby arugula leaves
3^1/$_2$ oz. smoked salmon pieces,
   sliced (see Note)

8 rounds of marinated goat
   cheese, drained
2 tablespoons roasted
   hazelnuts, coarsely chopped

In a large bowl, whisk together the oil and vinegar and season to taste.

Cut the avocado lengthwise into quarters, then discard the skin. Place an avocado quarter on each serving plate and arrange a small pile of arugula and smoked salmon on top.

Stack two goat cheese rounds on each plate and sprinkle with the hazelnuts. Drizzle with the dressing, season with black pepper, and serve.

Note: A whole smoked trout can be used instead of the salmon. Peel away the skin, remove the bones, then flake the flesh into bite-size pieces.

Serves 4

marinated baby octopus salad

1³/4 lb. baby octopus
4 tablespoons olive oil
2 garlic cloves, crushed
1 red bell pepper,
   thinly sliced

1 tablespoon sweet chili sauce
2 tablespoons chopped
   cilantro leaves
2 tablespoons lime juice

Using a small, sharp knife, carefully cut between the head and tentacles of each octopus, just below the eyes. Grasp the body and push the beak out and up through the center of the tentacles with your finger. Cut the eyes from the heads by slicing off a small disk. To clean the octopus heads, carefully slit through one side, avoiding the ink sac, and scrape out any guts from inside. Rinse well under running water and place in a large mixing bowl. Add the oil and garlic, mix well, then cover and marinate in the refrigerator for 1–2 hours.

When you're ready to eat, heat the grill or a charbroil pan to very hot. Cook the baby octopus, in batches if necessary, until just tender, about 3–5 minutes. Drain well on crumpled paper towels.

Put the bell pepper, sweet chili sauce, cilantro, and lime juice in a serving bowl, add the octopus, and mix together. Serve warm or cold.

Serves 4

Rich, eggy mayonnaise is the only kind to use here. Slathering delicate crustaceans with store-bought mayonnaise is a crime!

creamy seafood salad

5 cups conchiglie (pasta shells)
1 cup mayonnaise (see Note)
3 tablespoons fresh or 2 tablespoons dried tarragon
1 tablespoon finely chopped parsley
cayenne pepper, to taste
1 teaspoon lemon juice, or to taste
2 1/4 lb. peeled and shelled raw shellfish meat,
    such as shrimp, lobster, and crab (you could
    use any one of these, or a combination)
4 tablespoons olive oil
2 mild red radishes, thinly sliced
1 small green bell pepper, julienned

Cook the pasta in a large pot of boiling salted water until al dente. Drain, rinse under cold water, and drain again. Place in a large bowl and stir in 1–2 tablespoons of the mayonnaise. Allow to cool to room temperature, stirring occasionally to prevent sticking.

If using dried tarragon, simmer it in 3 tablespoons of milk for 3–4 minutes, then drain. Combine the tarragon, parsley, cayenne pepper, and lemon juice in a bowl with the remaining mayonnaise and mix well.

Meanwhile, preheat the grill or a charbroil pan to high. Toss the shellfish meat in the oil and cook until opaque, about 2–5 minutes, depending on the thickness. Remove from the heat, cut into bite-size pieces, and add to the pasta with the radish and bell pepper. Season to taste, then gently mix in the tarragon mayonnaise. Cover and chill, adding more mayonnaise or lemon juice before serving if needed.

Note: To make your own mayonnaise, whisk 2 egg yolks with 1 teaspoon of Dijon mustard and 2 teaspoons of lemon juice for 30 seconds or until light and creamy. Add 1 cup of light olive oil, a teaspoon at a time, whisking constantly—increase the amount of oil as the mayonnaise thickens. When all the oil has been added, stir in 2 teaspoons of lemon juice and season with salt and white pepper.

Serves 4

goat cheese, avocado, and
smoked salmon salad

charbroiled cauliflower salad with sesame dressing

2 heads baby romaine lettuce,
  leaves separated
1 1/2 cups watercress leaves
1 head cauliflower
12 garlic cloves, crushed
2 tablespoons vegetable oil
2 teaspoons sesame seeds,
  toasted
1 tablespoon finely chopped
  parsley

sesame dressing
3 tablespoons tahini
1 garlic clove, crushed
3 tablespoons seasoned rice
  wine vinegar
1 tablespoon vegetable oil
1 teaspoon lime juice
1/4 teaspoon sesame oil

Arrange the lettuce and watercress on a serving platter. Thoroughly whisk the sesame dressing ingredients together in a nonmetallic bowl with 1 tablespoon of water until well combined. Season to taste.

Preheat a charbroil pan to medium. Cut the cauliflower in half, then into 1/2-inch florets, and spread on a baking sheet. Mix together the garlic and oil, gently rub all over the cauliflower, and season well. Charbroil until golden on both sides and cooked through, about 2–3 minutes. Arrange over the lettuce and watercress, drizzle with the dressing, sprinkle with sesame seeds and parsley, and serve.

Serves 4 as a side salad

spicy tomato salad with sausage

3 tomatoes, diced
1 red onion, finely chopped
1 small green bell pepper, diced
2 tablespoons chopped cilantro

a few drops of hot pepper
  sauce, or to taste
8 thick gourmet sausages
crusty bread, to serve

Mix together the tomatoes, onion, bell pepper, cilantro, and some hot pepper sauce in a bowl. Cover and refrigerate for 1 hour, then allow to come to room temperature when you're nearly ready to serve.

Grill, broil, or pan-fry the sausages over medium heat for about 12 minutes or until nicely browned and cooked through, turning often. Set aside to cool, then cut into thick slices.

Arrange the sausages and the tomato mixture on four serving plates and serve with crusty bread.

Serves 4

Roast beef is just sublime piled on spinach and lavishly dressed with cool, creamy yogurt laced with horseradish and lemon.

roast beef and spinach salad with horseradish cream

horseradish cream
1/2 cup plain yogurt
1 tablespoon creamed horseradish
2 tablespoons lemon juice
2 tablespoons cream
2 garlic cloves, crushed
a few drops of hot pepper sauce, or to taste

2 cups green beans, trimmed
1 lb. sirloin steak
1 red onion, halved
1 tablespoon olive oil
2 cups baby spinach leaves
1 1/2 cups watercress leaves
1 1/3 cups sun-dried tomatoes

To make the horseradish cream, whisk all the ingredients in a small bowl with a little black pepper to taste. Cover and chill for 15 minutes.

Bring a pot of lightly salted water to a boil, add the beans, and blanch for 4 minutes or until tender. Drain, refresh under cold water, and drain again.

Meanwhile, preheat the broiler to high. Brush the steak and onion halves with the oil. Cook the steak for 2 minutes on each side or until seared but still rare, then remove from the heat, cover with foil, and leave for 5 minutes. (Cook the beef a little longer if you prefer it medium or well done.) While the steak is resting, cook the onion for 2–3 minutes on each side or until charred.

Toss the spinach, watercress, tomatoes, and beans in a large salad bowl. Slice the beef thinly across the grain, then layer over the salad. Thinly slice the broiled onion, add to the salad, and drizzle with the dressing. Season well with sea salt and freshly ground black pepper and serve.

Serves 4

roast beef and spinach salad with
horseradish cream

egg and spinach salad with croutons

2 slices whole-wheat bread,
    crusts removed
2 teaspoons vegetable oil
8 large spinach leaves, finely
    shredded
3 cups lettuce (see Note),
    finely shredded

3 scallions, finely sliced
1 cup sliced button mushrooms
2 tablespoons French dressing
3 hard-boiled eggs, peeled and
    quartered

Preheat the oven to 350°F. Brush the bread slices with the oil. Cut them in half, then into short fingers. Spread on a baking sheet and bake for 8 minutes or until golden. Set aside to cool.

Put the spinach, lettuce, scallions, and mushrooms in a serving bowl. Drizzle with the dressing and toss lightly to combine. Add the egg quarters and croutons, gently mix together, and serve at once.

Note: Any type of lettuce will suit this dish.

Serves 4 as a side salad

pasta salad with fresh vegetables

4 cups tricolor spiral pasta
2¹/2 tablespoons olive oil
2 cups broccoli florets
4 small yellow button squash
1 thin carrot, sliced diagonally

1¹/2 cups cherry tomatoes, halved
1¹/2 tablespoons lemon juice
1¹/2 tablespoons chopped
   parsley

Cook the pasta in a large pot of boiling salted water until al dente. Drain, rinse under cold water, and drain again. Transfer to a large serving bowl and gently mix with ¹/2 tablespoon of the oil to prevent sticking.

Put the broccoli and squash in a large pan of boiling water for 1 minute, then drain and plunge into ice water. Drain well, then add to the pasta with the carrot and cherry tomatoes.

Pour the lemon juice and remaining oil into a small screw-top jar and shake well. Pour over the salad, add the parsley, and mix well. Serve at room temperature.

Serves 4 as a side salad

Wonderfully soft eggplant absorbs the magical flavors of Morocco as it soaks up a wealth of warm, woody spices.

Moroccan eggplant with couscous

1 cup instant couscous
3/4 cup olive oil
1 onion, halved and sliced
1 eggplant
1 tablespoon ground cumin
1 1/2 teaspoons garlic salt
1/4 teaspoon ground cinnamon
1 teaspoon paprika
1/4 teaspoon ground cloves
3 tablespoons butter
2 large handfuls parsley, finely chopped
zest of 1 lemon
2 tablespoons capers, rinsed and drained

Put the couscous in a large bowl and add 1 1/2 cups boiling water. Let stand for 10 minutes, then fluff up with a fork.

Heat 2 tablespoons of the oil in a large frying pan and gently cook the onion for 8–10 minutes or until nicely browned. Remove with a slotted spoon, leaving the oil in the pan.

Cut the eggplant into $1/2$-inch-thick slices, then into quarters, and place in a large bowl. Mix the cumin, garlic salt, cinnamon, paprika, and cloves in a small bowl with $1/2$ teaspoon of salt, then sprinkle over the eggplant, tossing to coat well.

Heat the remaining oil in the frying pan over medium heat. Add the eggplant and cook, turning once, for 20–25 minutes or until browned. Remove from the pan and allow to cool.

In the same pan, melt the butter, then add the couscous and gently cook for 2–3 minutes. Stir in the onion, eggplant, parsley, lemon zest, and capers and remove from the heat. Cool to room temperature before serving.

Serves 4 as a side salad

Moroccan eggplant with couscous

watercress, feta, and watermelon salad

2 tablespoons sunflower seeds
1 lb. rindless watermelon, cut
   into 3/4-inch cubes
6 oz. feta cheese, cut into
   3/4-inch cubes
2 1/2 cups watercress sprigs

2 tablespoons olive oil
1 tablespoon lemon juice
2 teaspoons chopped oregano

Heat a small frying pan over high heat. Add the sunflower seeds and, shaking the pan continuously, dry-fry for 2 minutes or until the seeds are toasted and lightly golden.

Put the watermelon, feta, and watercress in a large serving dish and toss gently. Combine the oil, lemon juice, and oregano in a small bowl and season to taste with freshly ground black pepper (you probably won't need salt, as feta is usually quite salty). Pour the dressing over the salad and toss together well. Sprinkle with the sunflower seeds and serve.

Serves 4 as a side salad

cucumber salad with peanuts and chili

3 cucumbers
2 tablespoons white vinegar
2 teaspoons sugar
1–2 tablespoons sweet
 chili sauce
10 French shallots, chopped
 (see Note)

2 handfuls cilantro leaves
1 cup roasted unsalted peanuts,
 chopped
2 tablespoons crisp fried garlic
1 tablespoon fish sauce
 (optional)

Peel the cucumbers, cut them in half lengthwise, then scoop out the seeds and slice the flesh thinly.

Combine the vinegar and sugar in a small bowl and stir until the sugar has dissolved. Transfer to a large serving bowl and add the cucumbers, sweet chili sauce to taste, shallots, and cilantro. Mix gently, then cover and marinate in the refrigerator for 45 minutes. Just before serving, sprinkle the salad with peanuts, crisp fried garlic, and fish sauce.

Note: If French shallots are unavailable, use 2 red onions instead.

Serves 4 as a side salad

Lemon, thyme, parsley, and garlic lend a lip-smacking pungency to soft, creamy beans and beautifully rare tuna.

seared tuna and white bean salad

14 oz. fresh tuna steaks
1 small red onion, thinly sliced
1 tomato, seeded and chopped
1 small red bell pepper, thinly sliced
15-oz. can cannellini beans, rinsed and drained
2 garlic cloves, crushed
1 teaspoon chopped thyme
4 tablespoons finely chopped Italian parsley
vegetable oil, for brushing
2 cups baby salad leaves or baby arugula leaves
1 teaspoon lemon zest

warm vinaigrette
1 1/2 tablespoons lemon juice
4 tablespoons extra-virgin olive oil
1 teaspoon honey

Put the tuna steaks on a plate, sprinkle both sides with plenty of cracked black pepper, cover with plastic wrap, and refrigerate until needed. Nearer to serving time, toss the onion, tomato, and bell pepper in a large mixing bowl with the beans, garlic, thyme, and parsley.

To make the warm vinaigrette, put the lemon juice, oil, and honey in a small saucepan, bring to a boil, then simmer, stirring, for 1 minute or until the honey has dissolved. Remove from the heat but keep warm.

Brush the grill or a charbroil pan with a little oil and heat until very hot. Cook the tuna steaks for 1–2 minutes on each side, depending on their thickness—they should still be pink in the middle. Slice into large cubes and add to the beans. Pour the warm dressing on top and toss well.

Divide the beans and tuna between four serving plates. Top with the salad leaves, sprinkle with the lemon zest, and serve.

Serves 4

seared tuna and white bean salad

insalata caprese

3 large vine-ripened tomatoes,
    sliced
9 oz. bocconcini cheese, sliced
    (see Note)

16–20 whole basil leaves
3 tablespoons extra-virgin
    olive oil

Arrange alternating slices of tomato and bocconcini on a serving platter. Slip the basil leaves in between the tomato and bocconcini slices. Drizzle with the oil, season well with salt and ground black pepper, and serve.

Note: This popular salad is most successful when made with very fresh buffalo mozzarella, if you can find it. We've used bocconcini—small balls of fresh cow's milk mozzarella—in this recipe.

Serves 4 as a side salad

Moroccan spiced carrot salad

2 cardamom pods
1 teaspoon black mustard seeds
1/2 teaspoon ground cumin
1/2 teaspoon ground ginger
1 teaspoon paprika
1/2 teaspoon ground coriander
1/4 cup currants
4 tablespoons olive oil
1 tablespoon lemon juice

2 tablespoons orange juice
4 carrots
2 large handfuls cilantro,
    finely chopped
2 tablespoons finely chopped
    pistachio nuts
1/2 teaspoon orange flower
    water
1 1/2 cups plain yogurt

Crush the cardamom pods to extract the seeds; discard the pods. Heat a frying pan over low heat and dry-fry the mustard seeds for a few seconds or until they start to pop. Add the cardamom, cumin, ginger, paprika, and ground coriander and cook for 10 seconds or until fragrant. Remove from the heat and stir in the currants, oil, lemon juice, and orange juice.

Peel and coarsely grate the carrots. Put the grated carrots in a large bowl, stir in the spice mixture, then cover and set aside for 30 minutes. Mix into the chopped cilantro, pile the salad onto a serving dish, and sprinkle with the pistachios. Mix the orange flower water with the yogurt and serve separately, for people to help themselves.

Serves 4 as a side salad

Roasting garlic brings smoky notes and a deep, dark richness to this powerful little bulb. Leave the cloves unpeeled.

risoni and broccoli salad with roasted garlic

6 garlic cloves
1 tablespoon extra-virgin olive oil
4 tablespoons mayonnaise
4 tablespoons crème fraîche
3 tablespoons store-bought pesto
$1^1/_2$ tablespoons lemon juice
3 cups broccoli florets
10 oz. risoni (rice-shaped pasta)
$^2/_3$ cup toasted slivered almonds
1 tablespoon finely chopped parsley
1 tablespoon finely snipped chives
shaved Parmesan cheese, to serve

Preheat the oven to 350°F. Toss the whole, unpeeled garlic cloves in the oil and roast for 45 minutes or until soft and golden.

Gently squeeze the garlic cloves from their skins. Reserve four cloves as garnishes and place the remaining two cloves in a food processor with the mayonnaise, crème fraîche, pesto, and lemon juice. Process until just combined and set aside.

Steam the broccoli florets for 1–2 minutes or until just tender but still crisp, then refresh under cold water and drain well.

Bring a large pot of water to a boil. Add the risoni with 1 teaspoon of salt and cook for 8–10 minutes or until al dente. Drain well, then while the risoni is still warm, toss in a large bowl with the broccoli, roasted garlic dressing, almonds, parsley, and chives. Serve in deep salad bowls sprinkled with shaved Parmesan and topped with a roasted garlic clove.

Note: For a special touch for seafood lovers, mix in a handful of cooked peeled jumbo shrimp before serving.

Serves 4 as a side salad

insalata caprese

grilled tofu with broccoli and sesame dressing

3 cups broccoli florets
1/2 cup baby corn,
   halved lengthwise
3/4 cup snow peas, trimmed
1 large red bell pepper, sliced
7 oz. smoked tofu, cut into
   1/4-inch-thick slices

sesame dressing
3 tablespoons olive oil
2 teaspoons sesame oil
2 tablespoons lemon juice

Bring a pot of water to a boil and add a teaspoon of salt. Add the broccoli florets and cook for 30 seconds, then add the corn and snow peas and cook for 1 more minute. Drain, refresh under cold water, then plunge into a bowl of cold water to cool. Drain well and toss in a serving dish with the bell pepper.

Thoroughly whisk all the sesame dressing ingredients together in a small bowl. Pour half the dressing over the salad and toss gently to combine.

Heat the grill or a charbroil pan to medium. Add the tofu and cook for 2 minutes on each side or until grill marks appear. Add to the salad with the remaining dressing, toss gently, and serve.

Serves 4

red leaf salad

3 cups mixed red lettuce leaves
1 baby fennel bulb
1 small red onion
2 tablespoons olive oil
1 tablespoon balsamic vinegar

Wash and dry the lettuce leaves, then tear them into bite-size pieces.

Finely slice the fennel and onion and toss into a serving bowl with the shredded lettuce. Just before serving, drizzle the oil over the salad, then the vinegar. Toss lightly and serve.

Serves 4 as a side salad

Three types of rice lend an amazing texture to this salad, with each kind yielding a bite of its own—tender, firm, and nutty.

three-rice salad

1/2 cup long-grain white rice
1/2 cup short-grain brown rice
1/2 cup wild rice
1 small red bell pepper
1 small green bell pepper
3 tablespoons olive oil
1 garlic clove, crushed
1 1/3 cups frozen baby peas, defrosted
2 teaspoons lemon juice
pinch of mustard powder
3 tomatoes, peeled, seeded, and chopped
4 scallions, finely chopped
3 tablespoons finely chopped parsley
1/4 cup small black olives

Cook the rices separately, according to the packet instructions. Rinse, drain well, and set aside to cool.

Cut the bell peppers into large flat pieces and remove the seeds and membranes. Cook, skin side up, under a hot broiler until the skins blacken and blister. Allow to cool in a plastic bag, then peel away the skin and cut the flesh into thin strips. Gently toss in a bowl with the oil and garlic, then cover and marinate for at least 2 hours.

Cook the peas in a large pot of boiling salted water for 2 minutes, then refresh under cold water and drain. Put the bell pepper strips in a strainer and allow to drain over a bowl to collect the oil. Whisk the oil with the lemon juice and mustard powder and season to taste with salt and pepper.

Mix together the rice, bell pepper strips, peas, tomatoes, and scallions, then stir in the mustard dressing and parsley. Spoon onto a platter, sprinkle with olives, and serve.

Serves 4 as a side salad

grilled tofu with broccoli and sesame dressing

avocado and black bean salad

1¼ cups dried black beans
1 red onion, chopped
4 plum tomatoes, chopped
1 red bell pepper, chopped
13 oz. canned corn kernels,
    drained
1 bunch cilantro, roughly
    chopped
2 avocados, chopped
1 mango, peeled and chopped

1 bunch arugula, leaves
    trimmed

lime and chili dressing
1 garlic clove, crushed
1 small red chili, finely chopped
2 tablespoons lime juice
3 tablespoons olive oil

Soak the beans in cold water overnight. Rinse well, drain, and place in a large, heavy-based pot. Cover with cold water, bring to a boil, then reduce the heat and simmer for 1½ hours or until tender. Drain well and allow to cool slightly.

Put the beans in a large bowl with the onion, tomatoes, bell pepper, corn, cilantro, avocados, mango, and arugula. Gently toss to combine.

Whisk all the lime and chili dressing ingredients together in a small bowl. Pour over the salad, toss gently, and serve.

Serves 4

radicchio with figs and ginger vinaigrette

1 radicchio lettuce
1 small frisée
3 oranges (see Note)
1/2 small red onion, thinly
   sliced into rings
8 small green figs, quartered
3 tablespoons extra-virgin
   olive oil

1 teaspoon red wine vinegar
1/8 teaspoon ground cinnamon
2 tablespoons orange juice
2 tablespoons very finely
   chopped glacé ginger, with
   2 teaspoons syrup
2 pomegranates (optional),
   sliced in half

Wash the radicchio and frisée leaves thoroughly and drain well. Tear any large leaves into bite-size pieces and toss in a salad bowl.

Peel and segment the oranges, discarding all the bitter white pith. Add to the salad leaves with the onion and figs, reserving eight fig quarters. Whisk the oil, vinegar, cinnamon, orange juice, ginger, and ginger syrup in a small bowl. Season to taste, pour over the salad, and toss lightly.

Arrange the reserved figs in pairs over the salad. If you are using the pomegranates, scoop out the seeds, sprinkle over the salad, and serve.

Note: When in season, mandarins and mandarin juice are a delicious alternative to the oranges and orange juice in this salad.

Serves 4

This superb salad can be prepared ahead, then put aside until someone summons up the energy to fire up the grill.

spicy lamb and noodle salad

1 tablespoon five-spice powder
3 tablespoons vegetable oil
2 garlic cloves, crushed
2 lamb tenderloins (about
   9 oz. each)
1 lb. fresh Shanghai (wheat)
   noodles
1 1/2 teaspoons sesame oil
1 cup snow pea sprouts
1/2 red bell pepper,
   thinly sliced
4 scallions, thinly sliced
   diagonally

2 tablespoons sesame seeds,
   toasted

ginger and chili dressing
1 tablespoon finely chopped
   fresh ginger
1 tablespoon Chinese black
   vinegar
1 tablespoon Chinese rice wine
2 tablespoons peanut oil
2 teaspoons chili oil

Combine the five-spice powder, 2 tablespoons of the vegetable oil, and the garlic in a large bowl. Add the lamb and turn to coat well all over. Cover and marinate in the refrigerator for 30 minutes.

Cook the noodles in a large pot of boiling water for 4–5 minutes or until tender. Drain, rinse with cold water, and drain again. Add the sesame oil and toss to combine.

Meanwhile, preheat the grill or a charbroil pan to very hot and brush with the remaining vegetable oil. Cook the lamb for about 2–3 minutes on each side for medium-rare or until cooked to your liking. Remove from the heat, cover with foil, and let stand for 5 minutes, then thinly slice across the grain.

Whisk all the ginger and chili dressing ingredients together in a small bowl until well combined.

Put the noodles, lamb strips, snow pea sprouts, bell pepper, and scallions in a large bowl, pour the dressing over, and toss gently to combine. Sprinkle with the sesame seeds and serve immediately.

Serves 4

radicchio with figs and ginger vinaigrette

tofu salad

2 teaspoons sweet chili sauce
1/2 teaspoon grated fresh ginger
1 garlic clove, crushed
2 teaspoons soy sauce
2 tablespoons sesame oil
9 oz. firm tofu

1 cup snow peas, julienned
2 small carrots, finely julienned
1 1/2 cups finely shredded red
    cabbage
2 tablespoons chopped unsalted
    peanuts

Put the sweet chili sauce, ginger, garlic, soy sauce, and sesame oil in a small screw-top jar and shake well. Cut the tofu into 3/4-inch cubes and place in a bowl. Pour the marinade over, stir well, cover with plastic wrap, and refrigerate for 1 hour.

Put the snow peas in a small pan, add enough boiling water to cover, and blanch for 1 minute. Drain, plunge into ice water, and drain again.

Add the snow peas to the tofu with the carrots and cabbage and toss lightly to combine. Transfer to a serving bowl or individual plates, sprinkle with the chopped peanuts, and serve.

Serves 4

watercress salad

1 bunch watercress, washed
1 cucumber, peeled, halved,
    seeded, and thinly sliced
3 celery stalks, julienned
1 red onion, thinly sliced
    and separated into rings
1 bunch chives, snipped
3 oranges
1/2 cup chopped pecans
    or walnuts

mustard citrus dressing
3 tablespoons olive oil
3 tablespoons lemon juice
2 teaspoons grated orange zest
1 teaspoon seeded mustard
1 tablespoon honey

Pick the watercress into small sprigs, discarding the coarser stems. Toss in a large serving bowl with the cucumber, celery, onion, and chives.

Peel the oranges, removing all the bitter white pith, and cut the flesh into segments between the membrane. Add the segments to the salad.

Put all the mustard citrus dressing ingredients in a small screw-top jar, season with black pepper, and shake vigorously. Pour over the salad, toss, sprinkle with the nuts, and serve.

Serves 4 as a side salad

An intensely fresh blast of sharp, savory salsa swathes tender calamari and crisp greens in a snappy embrace.

calamari salad with salsa verde

1³/4 lb. small calamari, cleaned, scored, and sliced into 1¹/2-inch diamonds
2 tablespoons olive oil
2 tablespoons lime juice
1¹/4 cups green beans, trimmed and halved
1³/4 cups snow peas, trimmed
2 cups baby arugula leaves

salsa verde
1 thick slice white bread, crusts removed
²/3 cup olive oil
3 tablespoons finely chopped parsley
2 teaspoons finely grated lemon zest
3 tablespoons lemon juice
2 anchovy fillets, finely chopped
2 tablespoons capers, rinsed and drained
1 garlic clove, crushed

Toss the calamari in a bowl with the oil, lime juice, and a little salt and pepper. Cover with plastic wrap, refrigerate, and marinate for 2 hours.

To make the salsa verde, break the bread into chunks and drizzle with 2 tablespoons of the oil, mixing it in with your hands so it is absorbed. Place the bread and remaining oil in a food processor with the remaining salsa verde ingredients, and blend to a paste. If the mixture is too thick, thin it with a little extra lemon juice and olive oil to taste.

Bring a pot of lightly salted water to a boil, add the beans, and blanch until just tender, about 2–3 minutes. Remove with tongs, refresh under cold water, then drain well. Blanch the snow peas in the same pot for 1 minute, then drain, refresh in cold water, and drain again.

Meanwhile, preheat the grill or a charbroil pan to high. Cook the calamari in batches for 3 minutes per batch or until cooked. Take off the heat, allow to cool slightly, and toss in a bowl with the beans, snow peas, and arugula. Add 3 tablespoons of salsa verde and toss gently. Arrange on a serving platter, drizzle with the remaining salsa verde, and serve.

Serves 4

calamari salad with salsa verde

red cabbage salad

2¹/2 cups finely shredded
   red cabbage
2 cups finely shredded
   green cabbage
2 scallions, finely chopped
3 tablespoons olive oil

caraway dressing
2 teaspoons white wine vinegar
¹/2 teaspoon French mustard
1 teaspoon caraway seeds

Put the red and green cabbage in a large serving bowl with the scallions and mix together well.

Put all the caraway dressing ingredients in a small screw-top jar and shake well. Pour the dressing over the salad, toss lightly, and serve.

Serves 4 as a side salad

green bean and pine nut salad

2¼ cups green beans, trimmed
1 tablespoon olive oil
2 teaspoons lemon juice
1 tablespoon pine nuts

4 tablespoons tomato juice
1 garlic clove, crushed
a few drops of hot pepper
   sauce, or to taste

Bring a pot of lightly salted water to a boil, add the beans, and blanch for 2–3 minutes or until just tender. Drain, refresh under cold water, then drain again. Toss in a bowl with the oil and lemon juice.

Put a small frying pan over high heat. Add the pine nuts and dry-fry for 3–4 minutes or until the nuts are golden, shaking the pan frequently so they don't burn.

Put the tomato juice, garlic, and some hot pepper sauce in a small pan. Bring to a boil, then reduce the heat to low and simmer, uncovered, for about 8 minutes or until reduced by half. Allow to cool.

Arrange the beans on a serving plate, pour the tomato dressing over the top, and sprinkle with the toasted pine nuts.

Serves 4 as a side salad

Sesame seeds, sesame oil, and tahini open the door to a whole new world of flavor for wholesome soba noodles.

soba noodle salad with tahini dressing

2 1/2 cups yard-long beans or green beans
10 oz. soba noodles
4 scallions, finely sliced
1 tablespoon black sesame seeds

tahini dressing
1 1/2 tablespoons tahini
2 small garlic cloves, crushed
3 tablespoons rice vinegar
3 tablespoons olive oil
1 teaspoon sesame oil
2 teaspoons soy sauce
1 tablespoon sugar

Trim the beans and cut diagonally into long strips. Bring a pot of lightly salted water to a boil, add the beans, and blanch until just tender, about 2–3 minutes. Drain, refresh under cold water, then drain again.

Cook the noodles in a large pot of boiling water for 3–4 minutes or until tender. Drain, rinse under cold water, then drain again.

Put all the tahini dressing ingredients in a screw-top jar with 1 tablespoon of warm water and shake vigorously to combine. Season to taste.

Combine the beans, noodles, scallions, and sesame seeds in a large serving bowl. Add the dressing and lightly toss together just before serving.

Serves 4

soba noodle salad with tahini dressing

cabbage with crisp fried onion

½ Chinese or Savoy cabbage, finely shredded

½ cup crisp fried onion (see Note)

¼ cup crisp fried garlic (see Note)

½ red bell pepper, cut into very fine strips

3 tablespoons mint leaves, shredded

2 red chilies, finely sliced

4 lime wedges

dressing

4 tablespoons coconut milk

1 tablespoon fish sauce (optional)

1 teaspoon brown sugar

Arrange the cabbage on a serving platter and sprinkle with the crisp fried onion and garlic, bell pepper, and mint.

Combine the dressing ingredients in a small bowl and mix well. Pour over the salad, sprinkle with the chilies, and serve with lime wedges.

Note: Crisp fried onion and crisp fried garlic are available in jars from Asian markets. You can make your own by finely slicing peeled onion and garlic and deep-frying them in hot oil for about 30 seconds. Remove with a slotted spoon and drain on crumpled paper towels.

Serves 4 as a side salad

dill potato salad

4 all-purpose potatoes
2 eggs
2 tablespoons finely
   chopped dill
1¹/₂ tablespoons finely chopped
   French shallots

mayonnaise
1 egg yolk
2 teaspoons lemon juice
1 teaspoon Dijon mustard
¹/₃ cup light olive oil

Bring a large pot of water to a boil. Add the potatoes and cook for 20 minutes or until tender, adding the eggs for the last 10 minutes of cooking. Remove the potatoes and eggs from the pot and allow to cool.

Peel the potatoes, then cut into 1-inch cubes and place in a large bowl. Peel and chop the eggs and add to the potatoes with the dill and shallots. Gently toss to combine, then season.

To make the mayonnaise, put the egg yolk, lemon juice, mustard, and a pinch of salt in a food processor. With the motor running, gradually add the oil a few drops at a time. When about half the oil has been added, add the remaining oil in a thin, steady stream until it has all been incorporated. Gently stir the mayonnaise into the potato salad using a large metal spoon and serve.

Serves 4 as a side salad

Moroccan lamb salad

spice mix
2 garlic cloves, crushed
1 teaspoon ground cumin
1 teaspoon harissa (see Note)
1 teaspoon ground coriander

1/2 cup olive oil
2 large handfuls cilantro,
    finely chopped
2 tablespoons lemon juice
3 tablespoons chopped parsley
1/2 teaspoon ground turmeric
2 lamb tenderloins (11/4 lb.
    total), trimmed
1 cup plain yogurt
1 cup baby arugula leaves

pistachio couscous
1/2 cup orange juice
2 tablespoons lemon juice
1/2 teaspoon ground cinnamon
11/3 cups instant couscous
11/4 tablespoons butter
1/4 cup currants
heaping 1/3 cup chopped
    pistachios
15-oz. can chickpeas, rinsed
    and drained
3 tablespoons chopped parsley

In a small bowl, combine the spice mix ingredients. Put the oil in a large, nonmetallic bowl and stir in half the spice mix and all the cilantro, lemon juice, parsley, and turmeric. Mix well. Add the lamb, turning to coat well. Cover with plastic wrap and refrigerate for 1 hour.

Mix the remaining spice mix together with the yogurt, then cover and refrigerate until needed.

To make the pistachio couscous, pour the orange juice and lemon juice into a measuring cup, then add enough water to make 1 1/4 cups. Pour into a saucepan, add the cinnamon, and bring to a boil. Remove from the heat, pour in the couscous, cover, and let stand for 5 minutes. Add the butter and fluff up the couscous with a fork, raking out any lumps, then fold in the currants, pistachios, chickpeas, and parsley.

Meanwhile, preheat the grill or a charbroil pan to high. Drain the marinade from the lamb and cook for 2 minutes on each side or until charred on the outside but still pink in the middle. Remove from the heat, cover with foil, and let stand for 5 minutes, then slice across the grain.

Divide the couscous between four large serving plates and top with the arugula and lamb slices. Top with a dollop of the yogurt mixture and serve.

Note: Harissa is a fiery Middle Eastern chili paste readily available from specialty food stores.

Serves 4

Moroccan lamb salad

three-bean salad

1 cup green beans, trimmed and
cut into 1 1/2-inch lengths
1 1/4 cups frozen fava beans,
defrosted
8.5-oz. can lima beans, rinsed
and drained

10-oz. can red kidney beans,
rinsed and drained
1 small red onion, finely sliced
2 tablespoons chopped parsley
2 tablespoons French dressing

Bring a small pot of lightly salted water to a boil. Add the green beans and fava beans. Blanch for 1 minute, then drain. Refresh under cold water, then drain again.

Place the green beans and fava beans in a serving bowl with all the canned beans, onion, and parsley. Pour the dressing over and toss well.

Serves 4 as a side salad

roasted tomato and pasta salad with pesto

2/3 cup olive oil
4 cups cherry tomatoes
5 garlic cloves, unpeeled
5 cups orecchiette or other
   shell-shaped pasta

1/3 cup store-bought pesto
3 tablespoons balsamic vinegar
basil leaves, to serve

Preheat the oven to 350°F. Put 2 tablespoons of the oil in a roasting pan and warm in the hot oven for 5 minutes. Add the cherry tomatoes and garlic, season well, and toss until the tomatoes are well coated. Return to the oven and roast for 20 minutes (reserve the pan juices for the dressing).

Meanwhile, cook the pasta in a large pot of boiling salted water until al dente. Drain well and transfer to a large serving bowl.

Squeeze the flesh from the roasted garlic cloves into a bowl. Add the remaining oil, pesto, vinegar, and 3 tablespoons of the pan juices from the roasted tomatoes. Season with a little salt and pepper, then toss to combine. Add to the pasta and mix well to coat. Gently stir in the roasted tomatoes, then sprinkle with basil leaves. Serve warm or cold.

Serves 4

Succulent slices of juicy rare beef strike up a tender harmony with silky-smooth strips of eggplant.

charbroiled beef and eggplant salad

2 eggplants
2 tablespoons salt
3 zucchini, cut into 3/4-inch chunks
2 red bell peppers, sliced into 3/4-inch strips
1 1/4 cups button mushrooms, halved
2 onions, thickly sliced
3 tablespoons olive oil
1 tablespoon lemon juice
vegetable oil, for brushing
1 3/4 lb. sirloin steak, trimmed
1/2 cup snow pea sprouts
1 small handful shredded basil

Chop the eggplants in half lengthwise, then lay them cut side down and cut them into long slices about 1/2 inch thick. Spread the slices in a single layer on a plate and sprinkle with the salt. Set aside for 15 minutes, then rinse and pat dry thoroughly.

Meanwhile, toss the zucchini, bell peppers, mushrooms, and onions in a large bowl with the oil and lemon juice. Cover with plastic wrap and set aside for 30 minutes at room temperature.

Preheat the grill or a charbroil pan to high. Lightly brush with oil, add the beef, and cook for 2 minutes on each side to seal, turning once. Move the meat to a cooler part of the grill and cook for another 2 minutes on each side for medium-rare. Transfer to a plate and cover loosely with foil. Allow to cool, then slice thinly.

While the beef is resting, remove the vegetables from the marinade. Cook the vegetables and eggplant strips in batches on the barbecue for about 5 minutes each, or until just tender and browned.

Arrange a pile of snow pea sprouts on four serving plates. Top with the beef slices and vegetables, sprinkle with basil, and serve at once.

Serves 4

roasted tomato and pasta
salad with pesto

spaghetti, olive, and tomato salad

12 oz. spaghetti or
   bucatini pasta
2 large handfuls basil leaves,
   shredded
2 cups cherry tomatoes, halved
1 garlic clove, crushed
1/3 cup chopped black olives

3 tablespoons olive oil
1 tablespoon balsamic vinegar
1/3 cup grated Parmesan cheese

Cook the pasta in a large pot of boiling salted water until al dente. Drain, rinse under cold water, and drain again.

Toss the basil, cherry tomatoes, garlic, olives, oil, and vinegar in a serving bowl. Set aside for about 15 minutes to allow the flavors to develop, then mix in the drained pasta. Add the Parmesan, and salt and pepper to taste. Toss well and serve immediately.

Serves 4

easy grilled chicken and pasta salad

1 small grilled chicken
4 1/2 cups penne pasta
3 tablespoons olive oil
2 tablespoons white wine
   vinegar

2 cups cherry tomatoes, halved
1 large handful basil leaves,
   chopped
1/3 cup chopped black olives

Pull the meat and skin from the grilled chicken and finely shred it.

Cook the pasta in a large pot of rapidly boiling salted water until al dente.
Drain well, then transfer to a serving bowl. Combine the oil and vinegar
and toss through the pasta while it is still warm.

Add the shredded chicken, cherry tomatoes, basil, and olives and toss to
combine. Sprinkle with freshly ground black pepper and serve warm.

Serves 4

The humble chicken hits fresh new heights when given a dressing-down by a piquant salsa verde.

chicken with green chili salsa verde

green chili salsa verde
1 green bell pepper, roughly chopped
1–2 long green chilies, seeded and chopped
1 garlic clove, chopped
1 handful Italian parsley
1 handful basil
3 scallions, finely chopped
1 tablespoon lemon juice
1 tablespoon olive oil

4 boneless, skinless chicken breasts (about 7 oz. each)
$2^{1/3}$ cups watercress sprigs
3 celery stalks, sliced

To make the salsa verde, put the bell pepper, chilies, garlic, parsley, and basil in a food processor and blend to a purée. Transfer the mixture to a

sieve and allow to drain for 20 minutes, then transfer to a bowl and stir in the scallions, lemon juice, and oil. Season with salt and pepper.

Meanwhile, preheat the grill or a charbroil pan to medium. Add the chicken and cook for 6–8 minutes on one side. Turn and cook for an additional 5 minutes or until cooked through—the exact cooking time will vary depending on the heat of your grill and the thickness of the chicken breasts. Let cool slightly, then shred into a large bowl.

While the chicken is still warm, add the salsa verde and toss to coat well. Combine the watercress and celery in a serving dish, top with the chicken and salsa verde mixture, toss gently, and serve at once.

Serves 4

chicken with green chili salsa verde

coleslaw with lime mayonnaise

2¹/2 cups shredded red cabbage
2¹/2 cups shredded white
    cabbage
³/4 cup grated carrot
1¹/3 cups bean sprouts, trimmed
2 large handfuls cilantro leaves,
    finely chopped
3 scallions, finely sliced

lime mayonnaise

2 egg yolks
1 tablespoon soy sauce
1 bird's-eye chili, finely chopped
3 tablespoons lime juice
³/4 cup olive oil

Toss the red and green cabbage, carrot, bean sprouts, cilantro, and scallions together in a large bowl.

To make the lime mayonnaise, put the egg yolks, soy sauce, chili, lime juice, and a pinch of salt in a food processor. With the motor running, gradually add the oil a few drops at a time. When about half the oil has been added, add the remaining oil in a thin, steady stream until it has all been incorporated. Add 1 tablespoon of warm water and blend well.

Mix enough lime mayonnaise through the coleslaw to coat (any leftover mayonnaise can be refrigerated for 1 week). Refrigerate until ready to serve.

Serves 4 as a side salad

classic coleslaw

$1/2$ small green cabbage	$1/2$ red bell pepper, chopped
$1/4$ small red cabbage	3 scallions, sliced
2 carrots, coarsely grated	3 tablespoons chopped parsley
4 radishes, coarsely grated	$2/3$ cup mayonnaise

Remove the hard cores from the cabbages and shred the leaves with a sharp knife. Toss in a large bowl and add the carrots, radishes, bell pepper, scallions, and parsley. Refrigerate until ready to serve.

Just before serving, add the mayonnaise, season to taste with salt and freshly ground black pepper, and toss until well combined.

Serves 4 as a side salad

Sweet, juicy mango is the perfect partner to soft, flaky salmon and together they're pretty as a picture—a symphony in pink.

seared Asian salmon salad

1¹/₂ lb. salmon fillets
1 tablespoon olive oil
2 tablespoons lime juice
1 tablespoon soy sauce
2 tablespoons honey
2 ripe mangoes, peeled and
  thinly sliced
2 cups bean sprouts, trimmed
1 romaine lettuce, leaves
  separated
1 handful cilantro leaves

Asian dressing

1 tablespoon olive oil
1 tablespoon fish sauce
2 tablespoons lime juice
1 small red chili, finely chopped
¹/₂ teaspoon sugar

Remove any bones from the salmon and put the fillets in a single layer in a shallow nonmetallic dish. In a small bowl, whisk the oil, lime juice, soy sauce, and honey. Pour the mixture over the salmon, ensuring it coats all sides of the fish. Cover and refrigerate for 30 minutes.

Meanwhile, put all the Asian dressing ingredients in a small bowl and whisk until well combined. Set aside until needed.

Preheat the grill or a charbroil pan to high. If you like your salmon slightly pink in the middle, cook the fillets for 5 minutes on one side, then turn and cook the second side for another 4 minutes. If you prefer it cooked all the way through, cook for an extra minute on the second side. The exact cooking time will vary depending on the heat of your grill and the thickness of the salmon fillets. Let the salmon cool slightly, then break into chunks.

Put the mango, bean sprouts, and lettuce leaves in a serving bowl, add the salmon chunks, and toss gently. Pour over the dressing, sprinkle with the cilantro, and serve at once.

Note: Add the dressing just before serving so the bean sprouts and lettuce leaves don't become soggy.

Serves 4

seared Asian salmon salad

Greek salad

4 tomatoes, cut into wedges
1 hothouse English cucumber,
    peeled, halved, seeded, and
    diced into small cubes
2 green bell peppers,
    cut into strips
1 red onion, finely sliced

16 Kalamata olives
9 oz. firm feta cheese, cubed
3 tablespoons Italian parsley
12 mint leaves
1/2 cup olive oil
2 tablespoons lemon juice
1 garlic clove, crushed

Put the tomatoes, cucumber, bell peppers, onion, olives, feta, and half the parsley and mint leaves in a large serving bowl. Toss together gently.

Combine the oil, lemon juice, and garlic in a small screw-top jar, season well, and shake until thoroughly combined. Pour the dressing over the salad, toss well, and serve sprinkled with the remaining parsley and mint.

Serves 4 as a side salad

wild and brown rice salad

1/3 cup wild rice
2/3 cup long-grain brown rice
1 small red onion, finely diced
1/2 red bell pepper, finely
   chopped
1 celery stalk, thinly sliced
1 1/2 tablespoons chopped
   parsley
1/4 cup chopped pecans

citrus dressing
2 tablespoons orange juice
2 tablespoons lemon juice
1 teaspoon finely grated
   orange zest
1/2 teaspoon finely grated
   lemon zest
3 tablespoons olive oil

Cook the wild rice in a pot of boiling water for 30–40 minutes or until just tender. Drain well, then allow to cool. Meanwhile, boil the brown rice for 25–30 minutes or until just tender, then drain well and allow to cool. Toss all the rice in a bowl with the onion, bell pepper, celery, and parsley.

Put a frying pan over medium heat. Add the pecans and dry-fry, stirring often, for 2–3 minutes or until lightly toasted. Spread on a plate to cool.

Whisk all the citrus dressing ingredients together in a small bowl, pour over the salad, and gently fold through. Mix in the pecans just before serving.

Serves 4 as a side salad

Black vinegar adds a dark complexity to the dressing, bringing a savory depth to this crunchy salad.

Asian chicken salad with black vinegar dressing

1¼ lb. boneless, skinless chicken breasts
1 large carrot, julienned
2 cups baby Asian greens
1 cucumber, julienned
2 heaping cups bean sprouts, trimmed
3 scallions, sliced diagonally
1 small handful Thai basil leaves

black vinegar dressing
2 tablespoons black vinegar
2 tablespoons kecap manis
1½ tablespoons soy sauce
1 teaspoon sesame oil
2 tablespoons vegetable oil
2-inch piece of fresh ginger, peeled and grated

Heat the grill or a charbroil pan to medium. Add the chicken and cook for 6–8 minutes on one side. Turn and cook for an additional 5 minutes or until just cooked through—the exact cooking time will vary depending on the heat of your grill and the thickness of the chicken. Remove from the heat and let cool slightly.

Meanwhile, make the black vinegar dressing. Pour the vinegar, kecap manis, and soy sauce into a bowl and whisk together. Add the sesame oil and vegetable oil, whisk well, then stir in the ginger and set aside.

Shred or slice the chicken and toss in a serving bowl with the carrot, baby Asian greens, and cucumber. Pour over the dressing and toss gently. Sprinkle with the bean sprouts, scallions, and basil and serve.

Serves 4

Asian chicken salad with black vinegar dressing

spicy potato and bean salad

10 baby new potatoes, halved
1¹/₃ cups green beans, trimmed
    and halved diagonally

cilantro dressing
3–4 tablespoons olive oil
1 red chili, seeded and sliced
1 garlic clove, crushed
3 tablespoons chopped cilantro
3 teaspoons red wine vinegar
¹/₂ teaspoon caraway seeds

Put the potatoes in a large pot of gently simmering water and cook for 20 minutes or until tender but still firm. Drain and set aside.

Bring a pot of lightly salted water to a boil, add the beans, and blanch for 2–3 minutes or until bright green and just tender. Drain, refresh under cold water, then drain again. Put in a serving bowl with the potatoes.

To make the cilantro dressing, whisk all ingredients together in a small bowl until well combined. Pour the dressing over the potatoes, toss well, and serve at once so the salad doesn't discolor.

Serves 4 as a side salad

Waldorf salad

lettuce leaves, to serve
2 red apples, quartered
    and cored
1 large green apple, quartered
    and cored

1^1/2 celery stalks, sliced
^{1}/2 cup walnut halves
2 tablespoons mayonnaise
1 tablespoon sour cream

Line a serving bowl with lettuce leaves. Cut the apples into ^{3}/4-inch chunks and place in a large mixing bowl with the celery and walnuts.

In a small bowl, combine the mayonnaise and sour cream and mix well. Fold the dressing through the apple, celery, and walnut mixture, then transfer to the lettuce-lined serving bowl and serve at once.

Serves 4 as a side salad

Substantial yet summery, this one-pot wonder won't burst the seams of your itsy-bitsy, teeny-weeny, yellow polka-dot bikini.

potato and shrimp salad

5 waxy potatoes (such as red gold, rose fir,
    or fingerling), scrubbed
1½ lb. raw jumbo shrimp, peeled and deveined, tails intact
2 small bunches arugula, leaves trimmed
    and torn, or 3 cups baby arugula leaves
2 avocados, diced

red wine vinegar dressing
½ cup olive oil
3 tablespoons red wine vinegar
2 teaspoons mustard powder
2 tablespoons finely chopped dill

Put the potatoes in a large pot of salted water and bring to a boil. Reduce the heat and simmer rapidly for 12–15 minutes or until tender when pierced with a sharp knife. Drain well, allow to cool a little, then slice any large potatoes, keeping the small ones whole. Transfer to a serving dish.

Whisk all the red wine vinegar dressing ingredients together in a small bowl until thoroughly combined. Season with salt and black pepper and pour two thirds of the dressing over the potatoes. Toss gently and set aside.

Meanwhile, preheat the grill or a charbroil pan to high. Cook the shrimp for 2 minutes on one side or until just starting to turn pink. Turn them over and cook for another minute or until just cooked through. Add them to the potatoes along with the arugula and avocado. Top with the remaining dressing, toss gently, and serve at once.

Note: This salad can also be served cold. If you're making it in advance, dress the potatoes with two thirds of the dressing, but mix in the avocado, arugula, and remaining dressing just before serving.

Serves 4

potato and shrimp salad

fast melon salad

1 honeydew melon
1¹/₂ cups watercress sprigs
1 large avocado, sliced
1 red bell pepper, thinly sliced
5¹/₂ oz. marinated feta
   cheese, cubed
¹/₃ cup marinated Niçoise olives

dressing
2 tablespoons olive oil
1¹/₂ tablespoons white wine
   vinegar
1 teaspoon Dijon mustard

Cut the melon into slices and discard the rind. Arrange the melon slices on a large platter. Sprinkle with the watercress sprigs, then arrange the avocado, bell pepper, feta, and olives on top.

Put all the dressing ingredients in a small screw-top jar. Shake until well combined and drizzle over the salad.

Serves 4 as a side salad

green papaya salad

1 lb. green papaya, peeled and
  seeded (see Note)
2 small red chilies, thinly sliced
1 tablespoon brown sugar
1 tablespoon soy sauce
2 tablespoons lime juice
1 tablespoon crisp fried garlic
  (see Note)

1 tablespoon crisp fried shallots
  (see Note)
1/2 cup green beans, trimmed
  and cut into 1/2-inch lengths
8 cherry tomatoes, quartered
2 tablespoons chopped roasted
  unsalted peanuts

Grate the papaya into long, fine shreds with a grater or knife. Place in a large mortar with the chilies, sugar, soy sauce, and lime juice and lightly pound with a pestle until combined. Add the crisp fried garlic and shallots, beans, and cherry tomatoes. Lightly pound for another minute or two or until combined. Serve immediately, sprinkled with the peanuts.

Note: Green papaya and packets of crisp fried garlic and shallots are available from Asian markets.

Serves 4 as a side salad

Soft and fluffy on the inside, these scrumptious baked potatoes are loaded with tasty salad. Even the kids will love them.

baked potatoes filled with salad

4 large baking potatoes
  (about 12 oz. each)
4 slices prosciutto
11-oz. can corn kernels,
  drained
2 celery stalks, sliced
2 cups baby spinach leaves

dressing
2 1/2 tablespoons tomato juice
1 1/2 tablespoons red wine
  vinegar
2 tablespoons olive oil

Preheat the oven to 400°F. Thoroughly scrub the skins of the potatoes and prick them several times. Transfer to a roasting pan and bake, uncovered, for 1 hour or until tender when pierced with a sharp knife. (If you're in a hurry, you could microwave the potatoes on high, uncovered, for about 20 minutes, putting one potato in the center of the microwave and spreading the others out around it.)

Meanwhile, whisk all the dressing ingredients together in a small bowl. Season with salt and pepper and set aside.

Put a frying pan over high heat. Add the prosciutto and dry-fry for a few minutes on both sides or until nice and crispy. Break the prosciutto into small pieces and set aside.

Sit the potatoes on a chopping board and make two deep incisions crosswise over the top so they open out into quarters—be careful not to cut all the way through; the potatoes should still be attached at the base.

Put the corn, celery, and spinach in a large bowl, add two thirds of the dressing, and toss well. Put the potatoes on four serving plates and spoon a little dressing into each potato. Spoon the salad mixture into each potato, letting it spill over a little. Top with prosciutto and serve at once.

Serves 4

baked potatoes filled with salad

papaya and tamarind salad

1 green papaya, peeled,
    seeded, and grated
1/2 cup yard-long beans, sliced
1 garlic clove
1 small red chili, chopped
1 tablespoon dried shrimp
6 cherry tomatoes, halved
1 handful cilantro sprigs
2 tablespoons chopped roasted
    peanuts

tamarind dressing
2 tablespoons fish sauce
1 1/2 tablespoons tamarind purée
1 tablespoon lime juice
2 tablespoons brown sugar

To make the tamarind dressing, put all the ingredients in a small bowl. Mix well to dissolve the sugar and set aside. Put the grated papaya in a bowl, sprinkle with salt, and allow to stand for 30 minutes. Rinse well.

Blanch the beans in a pot of lightly salted boiling water until just tender, about 2–3 minutes. Drain and refresh under cold water, then drain again.

Pound the garlic and chili to a fine paste with a large mortar and pestle. Add the dried shrimp and pound until puréed. Add the papaya and beans and lightly pound for 1 minute. Add the tomato and pound briefly to bruise, then mix in the cilantro. Spoon onto four serving plates and pour the dressing on top. Sprinkle with the peanuts and serve.

Serves 4 as a side salad

green and wax bean salad

1^1/$_2$ cups green beans, trimmed   1 garlic clove, crushed
1^1/$_2$ cups wax beans, trimmed   shaved Parmesan cheese,
2 tablespoons olive oil   to serve
1 tablespoon lemon juice

Bring a pot of lightly salted water to a boil. Add the green and wax beans and blanch until just tender, about 2–3 minutes. Drain, refresh under cold water, then drain again.

Put the oil, lemon juice, and garlic in a bowl, season with salt and freshly ground black pepper, and mix well. Arrange the beans in a serving bowl, pour the dressing over, and toss to coat. Sprinkle with Parmesan and serve.

Serves 4 as a side salad

Olives and capers fire intense bursts of flavor into seductively salty haloumi, hosed down by cooling cubes of cucumber.

grilled haloumi salad with herb dressing

1 large cucumber, seeded and diced
3 tomatoes, seeded and diced
1/4 cup pitted and halved Kalamata olives
2 tablespoons capers, rinsed and drained
1 small red onion, finely diced
10 1/2 oz. haloumi cheese, cut into 1/2-inch slices

herb dressing
1 garlic clove, roughly chopped
1 small handful basil leaves
1 small handful Italian parsley
3 tablespoons olive oil
2 tablespoons lemon juice

Heat the grill or a charbroil pan to medium. While it is heating, prepare the salad: simply put the cucumber, tomatoes, olives, capers, and onion in a serving dish and mix together gently.

To make the herb dressing, crush the garlic with a mortar and pestle with a pinch of salt. Add the basil and parsley and pound until a paste starts to form. Add a little of the oil and pound for another 10 seconds. Stir in the remaining oil and lemon juice and season with black pepper. (If you prefer, purée the ingredients in a food processor.) Set aside.

Grill the haloumi for about 1–2 minutes on each side, or until it is starting to soften but not melt. Cut the haloumi into thick strips and arrange on top of the salad. Spoon the dressing over the top and serve at once while the haloumi is still hot, before it becomes rubbery and tough.

Serves 4

grilled haloumi salad with
herb dressing

ladies who lunch   Lingering over an elegant lunch with the ladies who matter the most to you can be a wicked and gossipy delight. Keep it fresh and keep it light, as a virtuous lunch leaves

plenty of room for one more glass of wine. Girly lunches are not just a luxury, but an essential element of a civilized way of life—a joyful celebration of female friendship.

Banish any notion of "ladies who lunch" as idle creatures with too much time and money and not enough to do. Lunching with your girlfriends is one of life's most sublime pleasures and a luxury available to all of us—an exploration of lives, loves, and longings. Even if your pals are a gaggle of good-time girls, chances are most of you will be watching your waistline. If there's a time to count calories, carbohydrates, and fat of all kinds this is it, so keep this chapter close at hand. All the recipes assembled within it are either low carb or low fat, specifically suited to the diet-conscious eater. You can enjoy these luscious salads to your heart's content, without sacrificing good taste on the altar of shapeliness. Dressing it up is another delicious aspect of putting on a girly lunch—if you've ever yearned to indulge your inner child, the one who secretly longs for something pretty in pink, this is the time to cut loose. Florals, pinks, and pretty napkins don't have to be fusty and faded, nor should delicate china be relegated to the back of the cupboard. Pull it all out and funk it up with a shot of intense color or search around for a pearly pink made fresh with a modish pattern. Whether you lean toward Jane Austen or Marilyn Monroe, there are myriad ways to make it pretty but keep it modern. Sacrifice is not a notion that should play a part in any celebration, even an everyday one. Moderation can be the enemy of variety and flavor, but you can make it tasty without being bad. Serve up salads and your girlfriends will thank you when they indulge in that extra glass.

scallop, ginger, and spinach salad

10 oz. scallops, without roe
vegetable oil, for brushing
2 cups baby spinach leaves
1 small red bell pepper, very
    finely julienned
heaping 1/2 cup bean sprouts,
    trimmed

sake dressing
2 tablespoons sake
1 tablespoon lime juice
2 teaspoons brown sugar
1 teaspoon fish sauce

Slice or pull off any veins, membranes, or hard white muscles from the scallops. Rinse the scallops and pat dry with paper towels. Put all the sake dressing ingredients in a small bowl and mix until the sugar has dissolved.

Heat a charbroil pan to high and lightly brush with oil. Cook the scallops in batches for 1 minute on each side or until just cooked.

Divide the spinach, bell pepper, and bean sprouts among four plates. Arrange the scallops on top, pour over the dressing, and serve at once.

Serves 4

Vietnamese shrimp salad

1/2 Chinese cabbage
1/2 red onion, finely sliced
1 lb. cooked tiger shrimp,
   peeled and deveined,
   tails intact
1 handful cilantro leaves,
   chopped
1 handful Vietnamese mint
   leaves, chopped

whole Vietnamese mint leaves,
   to serve

dressing
2 tablespoons sugar
2 tablespoons fish sauce
3 tablespoons lime juice
1 tablespoon white wine
   vinegar

Shred the cabbage finely and place in a large bowl. Cover with plastic wrap and chill in the refrigerator for 30 minutes.

Just before serving, put all the dressing ingredients in a small bowl with 1/2 teaspoon salt and mix well to dissolve the sugar.

In a serving bowl, toss together the shredded cabbage, onion, shrimp, cilantro, and chopped mint. Pour over the dressing, toss through gently, garnish with a few whole mint leaves, and serve.

Serves 4

Charbroiling tofu leaves it slightly chewy on the edges yet soft as silk inside, perfect for soaking up the earthy miso.

marinated tofu salad with ginger miso dressing

marinade
4 tablespoons tamari, shoyu, or light soy sauce
2 teaspoons peanut or vegetable oil
2 garlic cloves, crushed
1 teaspoon grated fresh ginger
1 teaspoon chili paste
1/2 teaspoon salt

ginger miso dressing
2 teaspoons white miso paste
2 tablespoons mirin
1 teaspoon sesame oil
1 teaspoon grated fresh ginger
1 teaspoon finely snipped chives
1 tablespoon toasted sesame seeds

1 lb. firm tofu, diced into 3/4-inch cubes
2 teaspoons vegetable oil
16 cups mixed salad leaves
1 cucumber, finely sliced
2 cups cherry tomatoes, halved

In a bowl, mix together all the marinade ingredients. Add the tofu and gently mix until well coated. Marinate for at least 10 minutes, or preferably for a few hours or overnight. When you're ready to cook, drain the tofu, reserving the marinade.

To make the ginger miso dressing, combine the miso paste with $1/2$ cup of hot water and leave until the miso dissolves. Add the mirin, sesame oil, ginger, chives, and sesame seeds and stir well until the mixture begins to thicken. Set aside.

Preheat a charbroil pan to medium. Brush with the oil, add the tofu, and cook, turning now and then, for about 4 minutes or until golden brown all over. Top with the reserved marinade and cook the tofu for another minute over high heat. Remove from the heat and allow to cool for 5 minutes.

Meanwhile, toss the salad leaves, cucumber, and tomatoes in a serving bowl. Add the tofu, drizzle with the dressing, toss well, and serve.

Serves 4

scallop, ginger, and spinach salad

roast duck salad with chili dressing

chili dressing
1/2 teaspoon chili flakes
2 1/2 tablespoons fish sauce
1 tablespoon lime juice
2 teaspoons brown sugar

1 Chinese roasted duck
1 small red onion, thinly sliced

1 tablespoon julienned
   fresh ginger
4 tablespoons roughly
   chopped cilantro
4 tablespoons roughly
   chopped mint
1/2 cup roasted unsalted cashews
8 butter lettuce leaves

To make the chili dressing, put the chili flakes in a frying pan and dry-fry over medium heat for 30 seconds, then grind to a powder with a mortar and pestle or spice grinder. Put the powder in a small bowl with the fish sauce, lime juice, and sugar; mix well to dissolve the sugar and set aside.

Remove the meat from the duck, cut it into bite-size pieces, and put it in a bowl. Add the onion, ginger, cilantro, mint, and cashews. Pour in the dressing and toss together gently.

Arrange the lettuce on a serving platter or use the leaves to line individual serving bowls. Top with the duck salad and serve.

Serves 4

shrimp and fennel salad

2³/4 cups raw jumbo shrimp,
    peeled and deveined
1 large fennel bulb (about
    14 oz.), thinly sliced
¹/2 large bunch watercress
2 tablespoons finely snipped
    chives

lemon and Dijon dressing
3 tablespoons lemon juice
¹/2 cup extra-virgin olive oil
1 tablespoon Dijon mustard
1 large garlic clove, finely
    chopped

Bring a large pot of water to a boil. Add the shrimp, return to a boil, and simmer for 2 minutes or until the shrimp turn pink and are cooked through. Drain and leave to cool. Pat the shrimp dry with paper towels, slice them in half lengthwise, and put in a large serving bowl. Add the fennel, watercress, and chives and mix well.

Whisk all the lemon and Dijon dressing ingredients together in a small bowl until well combined. Pour the dressing over the salad, season with salt and cracked black pepper, and toss gently. Arrange the salad on four serving plates and serve at once.

Serves 4

Fennel brings its wonderfully astringent bite to this salad,

lending an added piquancy to each forkful.

cannellini bean salad with fennel and tuna

3/4 cup dried cannellini beans
   (see Note)
2 fresh bay leaves, torn
1 large garlic clove, smashed
2 cups green beans, trimmed
1 baby fennel bulb, thinly sliced
1/2 small red onion, finely sliced
1 handful parsley leaves, chopped
1 tablespoon olive oil
10 oz. fresh tuna steaks

lemon and chili dressing
3 tablespoons lemon juice
1 garlic clove, finely chopped
1 red chili, seeded and finely
   chopped
1/2 teaspoon sugar
1 tablespoon lemon zest
4 tablespoons extra-virgin
   olive oil

Put the cannellini beans in a bowl, cover with plenty of cold water, and soak overnight, or for at least 8 hours. Rinse the beans well and put them in a large pot. Cover with plenty of cold water, add the bay leaves and garlic, bring to a boil, then reduce the heat and simmer for about 20–25 minutes or until tender. Drain.

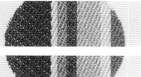

Meanwhile, bring another pot of lightly salted water to a boil, add the green beans, and blanch until just tender, about 2–3 minutes. Drain, refresh under cold water, then drain again. Gently toss in a serving bowl with the fennel, onion, and parsley.

Heat the oil in a large, heavy-based frying pan and cook the tuna steaks over high heat for 2 minutes on each side—they should still be pink in the center. Remove from the pan and let stand for 2–3 minutes. Whisk all the lemon and chili dressing ingredients in a small bowl until well combined. Season with salt and pepper.

Cut the tuna into 1¼-inch chunks. Add to the green beans with the cannellini beans, pour the dressing over, and gently toss to combine.

Note: To save time, you can use a 15-oz. can of cannellini beans instead of the dried beans. Leave out the first step and simply rinse and drain them well before adding them to the salad with the green beans.

Serves 4

roast duck salad with chili dressing

lentil salad

1/2 brown onion
2 cloves
1²/3 cups French green lentils
1 strip lemon zest
2 garlic cloves, peeled
1 fresh bay leaf
2 teaspoons ground cumin

2 tablespoons red wine vinegar
3 tablespoons olive oil
1 tablespoon lemon juice
2 tablespoons finely chopped
   mint leaves
3 scallions, finely chopped

Stud the onion with the cloves and put it in a pot with the lentils, lemon zest, garlic, bay leaf, 1 teaspoon of the cumin, and 3¹/2 cups water. Bring to a boil, then reduce the heat to medium and cook for 25–30 minutes or until the water has been absorbed. Discard the onion, lemon zest, and bay leaf, then finely chop the garlic cloves.

Put the chopped garlic in a bowl, add the vinegar, oil, lemon juice, and remaining cumin and whisk together well. Stir the mixture into the lentils along with the mint and scallions. Season well and set aside for 30 minutes to let the flavors develop. Serve at room temperature.

Serves 4 as a side salad

lamb, bell pepper, and cucumber salad

1 red onion, very thinly sliced
1 red bell pepper, very thinly
    sliced
1 green bell pepper, very thinly
    sliced
2 large cucumbers, julienned
4 tablespoons shredded mint

3 tablespoons chopped dill
vegetable oil, for brushing
1 1/4 lb. lamb tenderloin
4 tablespoons lemon juice
2 small garlic cloves, crushed
1/3 cup extra-virgin olive oil

Toss the onion, the red and green bell pepper, cucumbers, mint, and dill together in a large bowl.

Heat a charbroil pan or frying pan to medium. Lightly brush with oil and cook the lamb for 2–3 minutes on each side or until tender but still a little pink in the middle. Remove from the pan and let stand for 5 minutes. Thinly slice the lamb and gently mix it into the salad.

Combine the lemon juice and garlic in a small bowl, then whisk in the oil with a fork until well combined. Season with salt and black pepper, then gently toss the dressing through the salad. This is delicious served on fresh or toasted Turkish bread spread with hummus.

Serves 4

The sting of sweet heat, tender beef, and fresh, zesty salad

blows out the senses but not the waistline.

Thai beef salad

1¼ lb. beef tenderloin,
   trimmed
2 tablespoons fish sauce
1 tablespoon peanut oil
2 vine-ripened tomatoes,
   each cut into 8 wedges
½ butter lettuce, leaves
   separated

mint and chili dressing
1 small dried red chili, roughly
   chopped
4 tablespoons fish sauce
4 red Asian shallots, finely sliced
2 scallions, thinly sliced
   diagonally
4 tablespoons mint leaves
4 tablespoons cilantro leaves
1 garlic clove, crushed
⅓ cup lime juice
2 teaspoons brown sugar

Put the beef in a bowl and pour over the fish sauce. Cover and refrigerate for 3 hours, turning the meat several times to coat.

Put a baking sheet in the oven and preheat the oven to 425°F. Heat the oil in a frying pan and cook the beef over high heat for 1 minute on each side or until browned, then place on the hot baking sheet and roast for 15 minutes for medium-rare. Remove from the oven, cover loosely with foil, and set aside for 10 minutes.

Meanwhile, make the mint and chili dressing. Put a small, nonstick frying pan over medium-high heat. Add the chili and dry-fry for 1–2 minutes or until dark but not burned. Transfer to a mortar and pestle or spice grinder and grind to a fine powder. Place in a bowl with the remaining dressing ingredients, stirring to dissolve the sugar.

Thinly slice the beef and toss in a bowl with the dressing and tomatoes. Arrange the lettuce on a serving platter and pile the beef salad on top. Serve warm.

Serves 4

Thai beef salad

green salad with lemon vinaigrette

1 baby romaine lettuce
1 small butter lettuce
1 cup watercress leaves
1 small bunch arugula, trimmed

lemon vinaigrette

2 teaspoons finely chopped
   French shallots
1 1/2 teaspoons Dijon mustard
pinch of sugar

1 tablespoon finely chopped
   basil
1/2 teaspoon grated lemon zest
2 teaspoons lemon juice
1 tablespoon white wine
   vinegar
1 tablespoon lemon oil or
   olive oil
2 1/2 teaspoons olive oil

Separate all the lettuce leaves and rinse well. Rinse the watercress and arugula, then thoroughly drain all the salad greens. Pat dry and refrigerate.

To make the lemon vinaigrette, whisk the shallots, mustard, sugar, basil, lemon zest, lemon juice, and vinegar in a bowl. Mix the lemon oil and olive oil in a small bowl and slowly add to the dressing in a thin stream, whisking constantly to create a smooth, creamy dressing. Season to taste.

Put all the salad greens in a large bowl. Drizzle with the dressing, toss gently to coat, and serve at once.

Serves 4 as a side salad

tabbouleh

3/4 cup bulgur wheat
1 bunch mint
1 large bunch Italian parsley
   (see Note)
4 scallions, finely sliced
1 large tomato, finely chopped

2 garlic cloves, finely chopped
3 tablespoons lemon juice
4 tablespoons extra-virgin
   olive oil

Put the bulgur in a large bowl and add enough hot water to cover. Allow to soak for 15–20 minutes or until tender. Drain well and thoroughly squeeze out all the excess liquid.

Finely chop the mint and parsley and toss in a large bowl with the bulgur, scallions, and tomato.

Mix the garlic and lemon juice in a small bowl. Whisk in the oil and season to taste. Toss the dressing through the salad and serve.

Note: To vary this recipe you could halve the quantity of parsley and add 1 small bunch of arugula. To make the tabbouleh extra special, add 3 tablespoons of toasted pine nuts.

Serves 4 as a side salad

crab salad with green mango and coconut

dressing
2 garlic cloves, peeled
1 small red chili
1 1/2 tablespoons dried shrimp
1 1/2 tablespoons fish sauce
2 tablespoons lime juice
2 teaspoons brown sugar

4 tablespoons shredded
    coconut (see Note)
2 cups shredded green mango
    (see Note)
1 small handful mint leaves
    (torn if very big)

1 small handful cilantro leaves
2 kaffir lime leaves, shredded
1 1/2 teaspoons thinly shredded
    pickled ginger
12 oz. fresh crabmeat
4 small squares banana leaves
    (optional)
1/3 cup chopped toasted
    unsalted peanuts
4 lime wedges

Preheat the oven to 350°F. To make the dressing, pound the garlic, chili, dried shrimp, and 1/2 teaspoon salt to a paste with a mortar and pestle. Whisk in the fish sauce, lime juice, and sugar with a fork.

Spread the shredded coconut on a baking sheet and bake for 1–2 minutes, shaking the sheet occasionally to ensure even toasting. Watch the coconut closely, as it can burn easily.

Put the shredded mango in a large bowl and add the mint, cilantro, lime leaves, ginger, coconut, and crabmeat. Pour the dressing on top and toss together gently.

If using the banana leaves, place a square in each serving bowl (the leaves are for presentation only and are not edible). Mound some crab salad on top, sprinkle with the peanuts, and serve immediately with lime wedges.

Note: Freshly shredded coconut is delicious, so if you have the time, remove the skin from a coconut and shred the flesh using a vegetable peeler. For this recipe you will need about 3 green mangoes to get the right quantity of shredded mango flesh.

Serves 4

crab salad with green mango and coconut

charbroiled tomato salad

8 plum tomatoes
1$\frac{1}{2}$ teaspoons capers, rinsed and drained
4 basil leaves, torn
1 tablespoon olive oil
1 tablespoon balsamic vinegar
1 garlic clove, crushed
$\frac{1}{4}$ teaspoon honey

Cut the tomatoes lengthwise into quarters and scoop out the seeds. Heat a charbroil pan to medium and cook the tomato quarters for 1–2 minutes on each side or until grill marks appear and the tomatoes have softened. Cool to room temperature and place in a bowl.

Combine the capers, basil, oil, vinegar, garlic, and honey in a small bowl and season with salt and freshly ground black pepper. Pour the mixture over the tomatoes and toss together gently. Serve at room temperature with crusty bread and grilled meats.

Serves 4 as a side salad

Southwestern black bean salad

3/4 cup dried black beans
3/4 cup dried cannellini beans
1 small red onion, chopped
1 small red bell pepper,
    chopped
1¹/3 cups canned corn kernels,
    drained
3 tablespoons chopped cilantro

dressing
1 garlic clove, crushed
1/2 teaspoon ground cumin
1/2 teaspoon French mustard
2 tablespoons red wine vinegar
3 tablespoons olive oil

Put the black beans and cannellini beans in separate bowls, cover with plenty of cold water, and soak overnight. Rinse well, then drain and place in separate pots and cover with water. Bring both pots of water to a boil, reduce the heat, and simmer for 45 minutes or until the beans are tender. Drain, rinse, and allow to cool, then put all the beans in a serving bowl. Mix in the onion, bell pepper, corn, and cilantro.

To make the dressing, combine the garlic, cumin, mustard, and vinegar in a small bowl, then gradually whisk in the oil. Season lightly with salt and pepper. Pour over the bean mixture, toss lightly to combine, and serve.

Serves 4 as a side salad

Bathing the cucumber in a warm marinade imparts a tenderness rarely associated with this cool, crispy customer.

beef teriyaki with cucumber salad

4 beef tenderloin steaks
   (about 6 oz. each)
4 tablespoons soy sauce
2 tablespoons mirin
1 tablespoon sake (optional)
1 garlic clove, crushed
1 teaspoon grated fresh ginger
vegetable oil, for brushing
1 teaspoon sugar
1 teaspoon toasted sesame seeds

cucumber salad
1 large cucumber, peeled,
   seeded, and diced
1/2 red bell pepper, diced
2 scallions, thinly sliced
   diagonally
2 teaspoons sugar
1 tablespoon rice wine vinegar

Put the beef steaks side by side in a large dish. Combine the soy sauce, mirin, sake, garlic, and ginger and pour over the steaks, turning to coat. Cover and refrigerate for at least 30 minutes, turning once or twice.

To make the cucumber salad, toss the cucumber, bell pepper, and scallions in a bowl. Put the sugar and rice wine vinegar in a saucepan with

3 tablespoons of water and stir over medium heat until the sugar has dissolved. Increase the heat and simmer for 3–4 minutes or until the mixture has thickened. Pour over the cucumber salad, stir to combine, and allow to cool completely.

Heat a charbroil pan or grill to high and brush with a little oil. Drain the beef steaks, reserving the marinade. Cook the steak for 4 minutes on each side or until done to your liking. Remove from the heat, cover with foil, and allow to stand in a warm place for 5–10 minutes.

Put the sugar and the reserved marinade in a saucepan and heat, stirring, until the sugar has dissolved. Bring to a boil and simmer for 2 minutes. Take off the heat, but keep warm.

Slice each tenderloin into 1/2-inch strips and arrange on four serving plates. Spoon some of the marinade and cucumber salad on top and sprinkle with the sesame seeds. Serve with steamed rice.

Serves 4

charbroiled tomato salad

chickpea and olive salad

1¹/2 cups dried chickpeas
1 cucumber
2 tomatoes, seeded and cut
    into ¹/2-inch cubes
1 small red onion, finely chopped
3 tablespoons chopped parsley
¹/2 cup pitted black olives

lemon and garlic dressing
1 tablespoon lemon juice
3 tablespoons olive oil
1 garlic clove, crushed
1 teaspoon honey

Cover the chickpeas in plenty of cold water and soak overnight. Drain well, put them in a pot, and cover with cold water. Bring to a boil, then reduce the heat and simmer for 25 minutes or until just tender. Drain and allow to cool, then place in a serving bowl.

Cut the cucumber in half lengthwise, scoop out the seeds, and cut the flesh into ¹/2-inch chunks. Add to the chickpeas with the tomatoes, onion, parsley, and olives. Put all the lemon and garlic dressing ingredients in a small screw-top jar, shake well, and pour over the salad. Toss lightly to combine and serve at room temperature.

Serves 4 as a side salad

salata baladi

1 1/2 tablespoons extra-virgin
    olive oil
1 1/2 tablespoons lemon juice
1 baby romaine lettuce,
    leaves torn
2 ripe tomatoes, each cut into
    8 wedges
1 small green bell pepper, cut
    into bite-size pieces

2 small cucumbers, seeded
    and chopped
4 radishes, sliced
1 small sweet onion (such as
    Vidalia) or red onion, thinly
    sliced
2 tablespoons chopped Italian
    parsley
1 small handful mint leaves

In a bowl, whisk together the oil and lemon juice. Season well with salt and freshly ground black pepper.

Put all the vegetables and herbs in a large serving bowl and toss together well. Add the dressing and toss again. Serve at once, while the salad is crisp.

Serves 4 as a side salad

The simplest lemon vinaigrette and a sprinkling of parsley bring out the true, sweet flavor of superbly fresh seafood.

seafood salad

1 lb. small calamari
2¹/4 lb. large clams (vongole)
2¹/4 lb. black mussels
1 lb. raw shrimp, peeled and
    deveined, tails intact
2 handfuls Italian parsley, finely
    chopped

dressing
2 tablespoons lemon juice
4 tablespoons olive oil
1 garlic clove, crushed

To clean the calamari, gently pull the tentacles away from the hoods (the intestines should come away at the same time). Remove the intestines from the tentacles by cutting under the eyes, then remove the beak if it remains in the center of the tentacles by using your fingers to push up the center. Pull away the soft bones (quill) from the hoods. Rub the hoods under cold running water and the skin should come away easily. Rinse well, then slice the calamari into rings and roughly chop the tentacles.

Scrub the clams and mussels with a stiff brush and pull out the hairy beards. Discard any that are cracked or any open ones that don't close when tapped on the counter. Rinse well under running water. Fill a pot with ³/4 inch of water and add the clams and mussels. Cover and boil for 4–5 minutes or until the shells open. Remove, reserving the liquid, and discard any that do not open. Remove the mussels and clams from their shells and place them in a bowl.

Bring 4 cups of water to a boil, then add the shrimp and calamari. Simmer for 3–4 minutes or until the shrimp turn pink and the calamari is tender. Drain and add to the clams and mussels.

In a small bowl, whisk all the dressing ingredients together. Season to taste and pour over the seafood. Add 4 tablespoons of the parsley, gently toss to coat, then cover and refrigerate for 30–40 minutes. Just before serving, sprinkle with the remaining parsley.

Serves 4

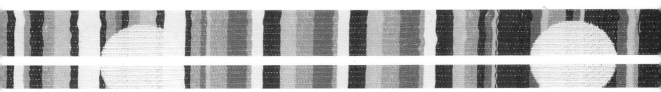

salata baladi

citrus, sugar snap pea, and walnut salad

2 oranges
2 small grapefruit
1 cup sugar snap peas
1/2 bunch arugula, leaves torn
1/2 oak leaf lettuce, leaves torn
1 cucumber, sliced
4 tablespoons walnut pieces

walnut dressing
2 tablespoons walnut oil
2 tablespoons vegetable oil
2 teaspoons tarragon vinegar
2 teaspoons seeded mustard
1 teaspoon sweet chili sauce

Peel the rind and bitter white pith from the oranges and grapefruit. Cut the flesh into segments between the membranes, removing the seeds. Place the segments in a large serving bowl.

Trim the sugar snap peas, put them in a pot, and cover with boiling water. Allow to stand for 2 minutes, then refresh under cold water. Drain and pat dry with paper towels and add to the citrus segments with the arugula, lettuce, cucumber, and walnut pieces.

Put all the walnut dressing ingredients in a screw-top jar and shake well to combine. Pour the dressing over the salad, toss well, and serve.

Serves 4 as a side salad

shrimp and papaya salad with lime dressing

1¹/₂ lb. cooked shrimp
1 large papaya, peeled, seeded,
   and chopped
1 small red onion, finely sliced
2 celery stalks, finely sliced
2 tablespoons shredded mint

lime dressing
¹/₂ cup vegetable oil
3 tablespoons lime juice
2 teaspoons finely grated
   fresh ginger
1 teaspoon superfine sugar

Peel the shrimp, leaving the tails intact. Gently pull out the dark vein from each shrimp back, starting at the head. Put the shrimp in a bowl.

Whisk all the lime dressing ingredients together in a small bowl. Season to taste with salt and freshly ground black pepper, then pour over the shrimp and gently toss to coat. Add the papaya, onion, celery, and mint and gently toss to combine. Serve the salad at room temperature, or cover and refrigerate for up to 3 hours before serving.

Serves 4

Poaching calamari in a fragrant broth scented with lemongrass and lime leaves renders it delicate, tender, and aromatic.

calamari salad

lime and ginger dressing
2 large garlic cloves, crushed
2 teaspoons grated fresh ginger
3 small red chilies, seeded
    and thinly sliced
2 tablespoons brown sugar
2 tablespoons fish sauce
2 tablespoons lime juice
1/2 teaspoon sesame oil

1 lb. cleaned calamari tubes
6 kaffir lime leaves
1 stem lemongrass, white part
    only, chopped
3–4 red Asian shallots, thinly sliced
1 cucumber, cut in half
    lengthwise, seeded, and
    thinly sliced
3 tablespoons chopped cilantro
4 tablespoons mint leaves
crisp fried red Asian shallot
    flakes, to serve

Put the lime and ginger dressing ingredients in a small pan with 1 tablespoon of water. Stir over low heat until the sugar has dissolved. Set aside.

Cut the calamari tubes in half lengthwise and rinse under running water. Score a crisscross pattern on the inside of the calamari, taking care not to cut all the way through, then cut into 1¼-inch pieces.

Put the lime leaves and lemongrass in a pot with 5 cups water. Bring to a boil, reduce the heat, and simmer for 5 minutes. Add half the calamari and cook for 30 seconds, or until they begin to curl up and turn opaque. Remove with a slotted spoon and keep warm. Repeat with the remaining calamari, then discard the liquid, lime leaves, and lemongrass.

Put the calamari, shallots, cucumber, cilantro, and mint in a large bowl, then add the dressing and toss together well. Sprinkle with the fried shallot flakes and serve.

Serves 4

calamari salad

escabeche

1 lb. skinless fish fillets,
     such as catfish, haddock,
     halibut, or monkfish
seasoned all-purpose flour
1/3 cup extra-virgin olive oil
1 red onion, thinly sliced
2 garlic cloves, thinly sliced
2 thyme sprigs
1 teaspoon ground cumin
2 scallions, sliced

1/2 teaspoon finely grated
     orange zest
3 tablespoons orange juice
3/4 cup white wine
3/4 cup white wine vinegar
1/2 cup pitted green olives,
     roughly chopped
1/2 teaspoon superfine sugar

Dust the fish lightly with the flour. Heat 2 tablespoons of the oil in a frying pan over medium heat and cook the fish in batches for 2–3 minutes on each side or until lightly browned and cooked through. Place in a single layer in a large, shallow, nonmetallic dish.

Heat the remaining oil in the same pan. Add the onion and garlic and cook, stirring, over medium heat for 5 minutes or until soft. Add the thyme, cumin, and scallions and stir until fragrant, then add the remaining ingredients and season to taste. Bring to a boil, then pour the liquid over the fish. Allow the fish to cool in the liquid, or refrigerate overnight. Serve at room temperature, on a bed of watercress or salad greens.

Serves 4

scallop seviche

16 scallops, on the half shell
1 teaspoon finely grated lime
   zest, plus extra strips of lime
   zest, to serve
2 garlic cloves, chopped

2 small red chilies, seeded and
   finely chopped
1/2 cup lime juice
1–2 tablespoons chopped parsley
1 tablespoon olive oil

Remove the scallops from their shells and reserve the shells. You may need to use a small, sharp knife to slice the scallops free—be careful not to leave any scallop meat behind. Slice or pull off any veins, membranes, or hard white muscles, leaving any roe attached. Rinse the scallops and pat them dry with paper towels.

In a large nonmetallic bowl, mix together the remaining ingredients and season with salt and freshly ground black pepper. Add the scallops and gently stir to coat. Cover with plastic wrap and refrigerate for 2 hours or up to 1 day—during this time the acid in the lime juice will "cook" the scallops, firming the flesh and turning it opaque.

To serve, slide each scallop back onto a half shell and spoon the dressing on top. Sprinkle with the lime zest strips and enjoy cold as a starter salad.

Serves 4

When the occasion calls for a bit of flair, this salad has all the flashiness of flamenco and sings of siestas in the sun.

Spanish-style seafood salad

1 lb. raw shrimp
5 oz. scallops, with roe
12 black mussels
2 slices of lemon
2 fresh or dried bay leaves
pinch of dried thyme
3 cups broccoli florets
2 teaspoons capers, rinsed
    and drained
16 dry-cured black olives

2 scallions, chopped
1/2 small green bell pepper,
    diced

dressing
2 tablespoons olive oil
1 1/2 tablespoons lemon juice
1 teaspoon Dijon mustard
1 garlic clove, crushed

Peel the shrimp and pull out the dark vein from each shrimp back, starting at the head. Slice or pull off any veins, membranes, or hard white muscles from the scallops, leaving any roe attached. Rinse the scallops and pat them dry with paper towels.

Scrub the mussels with a stiff brush and pull out the hairy beards. Discard any broken mussels or any open ones that don't close when tapped on the counter. Rinse well under running water.

Put the lemon slices, bay leaves, and thyme in a large pot with 3 cups water. Bring to a boil. Add the scallops and cook for 30 seconds or until opaque. Remove with a slotted spoon and drain on crumpled paper towels. Add the shrimp and cook for 2–3 minutes or until opaque. Remove with a slotted spoon and drain on paper towels.

Add the mussels to the pan, cover, and cook for 4–5 minutes or until they open, shaking the pan occasionally. Drain the mussels on crumpled paper towels, discarding any that haven't opened. Discard one half shell from each mussel and put all the seafood in a serving bowl.

Blanch the broccoli in a pot of boiling water for 2 minutes. Refresh in cold water, then drain and add to the seafood with the capers, olives, scallions, and bell pepper.

Whisk the dressing ingredients in a small bowl with some salt and freshly ground black pepper. Pour over the seafood and gently toss to coat. Cover and refrigerate for about 2 hours before serving.

Serves 4

scallop seviche

smoked trout with chili raspberry dressing

2 bunches sorrel
1 small smoked trout
12 asparagus spears, trimmed
1 small red onion, thinly sliced
1 1/2 cups pear tomatoes, halved
5 1/2-oz. carton raspberries

chili raspberry dressing
1 cup raspberries
1/2 teaspoon chili paste
1 garlic clove, crushed
4 tablespoons olive oil
1 1/2 tablespoons raspberry
    vinegar or white wine
    vinegar

Trim the stalks from the sorrel, rinse the leaves well, pat them dry, and put in the refrigerator to crisp. Peel away and discard the skin and bones from the trout. Break the flesh into pieces.

Put the chili raspberry dressing ingredients in a small pan over low heat until the raspberries begin to break up and color the liquid. Transfer to a bowl, whisk well, and season with salt and freshly ground black pepper.

Boil, steam, or microwave the asparagus until just tender, then drain and refresh under cold water. Drain again. Divide the sorrel between individual plates. Arrange the asparagus, trout, onion, tomatoes, and raspberries on top, drizzle with the dressing, and serve.

Serves 4

roasted cherry tomato and chicken salad

9-oz. carton cherry tomatoes or
   small truss tomatoes
2 whole garlic cloves, unpeeled
1 tablespoon olive oil
1 thyme sprig, cut into 3 pieces

1 grilled chicken
2 cups baby arugula leaves
2 tablespoons capers, rinsed and
   drained (optional)
1 tablespoon balsamic vinegar

Preheat the oven to 350°F. Put the tomatoes, whole garlic cloves, oil, and thyme in a roasting pan and bake for 15 minutes.

Meanwhile, remove the meat from the chicken, discarding the skin and bones. Shred the meat and toss in a bowl with the arugula and capers.

Allow the cooked tomatoes to cool slightly, then gently squash each one to release some of the juice. Add the tomatoes to the chicken mixture, leaving the garlic and pan juices in the roasting dish. Discard the thyme. Squeeze the flesh from each roasted garlic clove and mix with any pan juices. Add the vinegar and mix again. Pour the mixture over the salad, toss gently, and serve.

Serves 4

A deeply satisfying dish that is a treat for the lips and kind to the hips, and healthy through and through.

brown rice and lentils with pine nuts and spinach

2/3 cup brown rice
3 tablespoons extra-virgin
  olive oil
1 small red onion, diced
2 garlic cloves, crushed
1 small carrot, diced
1 1/2 celery stalks, diced
2/3 cup French green lentils (see
  Note)

2 small tomatoes, seeded
  and diced
2 tablespoons chopped cilantro
2 tablespoons chopped mint
1 1/2 tablespoons balsamic
  vinegar
1 tablespoon lemon juice
2 tablespoons toasted pine nuts
2 heaping cups baby spinach
  leaves

Bring a large pot of water to a boil. Add 1 teaspoon of salt and the rice, then cook for 20 minutes or until tender. Drain well, then rinse the rice under cold running water.

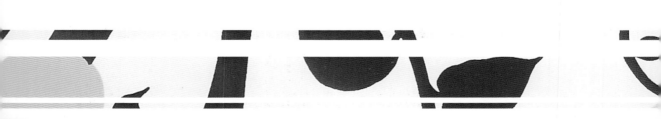

Heat 2 tablespoons of the oil in a saucepan and fry the onion, garlic, carrot, and celery over low heat for 5 minutes or until softened. Add the lentils and 1 1/2 cups of water. Bring to a boil, then reduce the heat and simmer for 15 minutes or until tender. Drain well, but do not rinse. Place in a large bowl with the rice, tomatoes, cilantro, and mint.

Whisk the remaining oil with the vinegar and lemon juice and season well with salt and freshly ground black pepper. Pour the dressing over the lentils, add the pine nuts and spinach, toss well and serve.

Note: If you are unable to obtain French green lentils, you can use green or brown lentils instead.

Serves 4 as a side salad

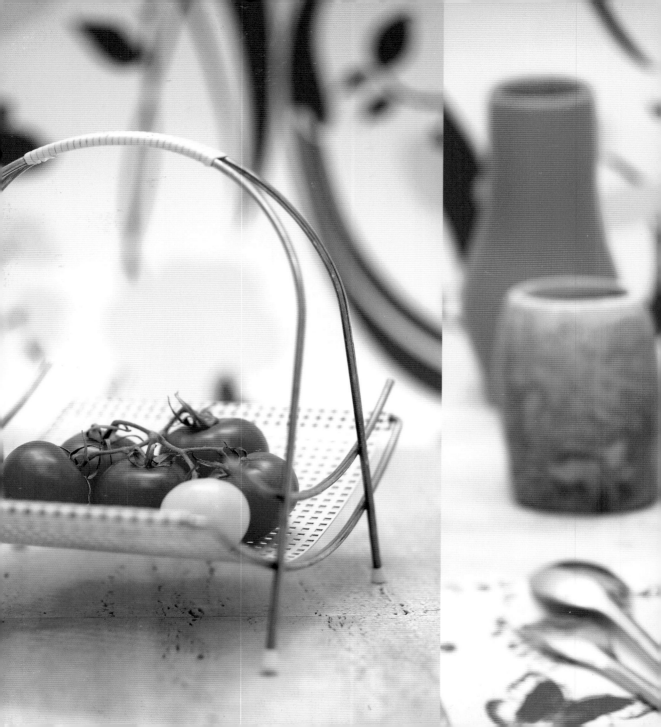

roasted cherry tomato and chicken salad

Thai noodle salad

9 oz. dried instant egg noodles
1 lb. cooked jumbo shrimp,
    peeled and deveined,
    tails intact
5 scallions, sliced
2 tablespoons chopped cilantro
1 red bell pepper, diced
1 cup snow peas, julienned
4 lime wedges

dressing
2 tablespoons grated
    fresh ginger
2 tablespoons soy sauce
2 tablespoons sesame oil
4 tablespoons red wine vinegar
1 tablespoon sweet chili sauce
2 garlic cloves, crushed
4 tablespoons kecap manis

Cook the egg noodles in a pot of boiling water for 2 minutes or until tender. Drain thoroughly, then allow to cool in a large serving bowl.

Whisk all the dressing ingredients together in a small bowl and gently mix through the cooled noodles. Add the shrimp, scallions, cilantro, bell pepper, and snow peas. Toss gently and serve with lime wedges.

Serves 4

marinated fish salad with chili and basil

1 lb. skinless firm whitefish
    fillets
3 tablespoons lime juice
3 tablespoons light coconut milk
mixed salad leaves, to serve
3 tomatoes, diced
3 cucumbers, diced

5 scallions, finely sliced
2 red chilies, seeded and sliced
2 garlic cloves, crushed
1 teaspoon grated fresh ginger
1 large handful basil leaves,
    chopped

Slice the fish into thin strips and place in a nonmetallic bowl. Put the lime juice and coconut milk in a small bowl with 1 teaspoon salt and $1/4$ teaspoon cracked black pepper. Mix well, then pour over the fish. Cover and refrigerate for several hours or overnight, turning once or twice. (The acid in the lime juice will "cook" the fish, firming the flesh and turning it opaque.)

Arrange some salad leaves on four serving plates. Gently mix the tomatoes, cucumbers, scallions, chilies, garlic, and ginger into the fish, spoon over the salad leaves, and serve.

Note: When mangoes are in season, peel and roughly dice the flesh of 1 mango and toss it through the finished salad for extra flavor and sweetness.

Serves 4

The toasty, exotic allure of sesame always promises good food to come. These noodles are light yet utterly ravishing.

somen noodle salad with sesame dressing

sesame dressing
3 tablespoons toasted
  sesame seeds
2¹/₂ tablespoons shoyu or light
  soy sauce
2 tablespoons rice vinegar
2 teaspoons sugar
¹/₂ teaspoon grated fresh ginger
¹/₂ teaspoon dashi granules

4¹/₂ oz. dried somen noodles
1 cup snow peas, trimmed and
  finely sliced diagonally
1 cup julienned daikon radish
1 small carrot, julienned
1 scallion, sliced diagonally
1 heaping cup baby spinach
  leaves
2 teaspoons toasted sesame
  seeds

To make the sesame dressing, put the sesame seeds in a mortar and grind with a pestle until fine and moist. Combine the soy sauce, vinegar, sugar, ginger, and dashi granules in a small saucepan with $1/2$ cup water and bring to a boil. Reduce the heat to medium and simmer, stirring, for 2 minutes or until the dashi granules have dissolved. Remove from the heat and allow to cool. Gradually mix in the ground sesame seeds, stirring to form a thick dressing.

Cook the noodles in a large pot of boiling water for 2 minutes or until tender. Drain, rinse under cold water, and allow to cool completely. Cut the noodles into 4-inch lengths using scissors.

Put the snow peas in a large, shallow serving bowl with the daikon, carrot, scallion, spinach, and noodles. Add the dressing and toss well to combine, then cover and refrigerate until ready to serve. Just before serving, sprinkle with the toasted sesame seeds.

Serves 4

Thai noodle salad

garden salad

½ bunch green oak leaf lettuce
1 bunch arugula, trimmed
1 small radicchio lettuce
1 green bell pepper,
    cut into thin strips
zest of 1 lemon

dressing
1 tablespoon roughly
    chopped cilantro
1½ tablespoons lemon juice
1 teaspoon brown sugar
1 tablespoon olive oil
1 garlic clove, crushed (optional)

Wash and dry the salad greens thoroughly, then tear into bite-size pieces. Toss in a large serving bowl with the bell pepper and lemon zest.

Whisk the dressing ingredients in a small bowl until the sugar has dissolved. Just before serving, pour the dressing over the salad and toss well.

Serves 4 as a side salad

cranberry bean, beet, and mint salad

15-oz. can cranberry beans,
    drained and rinsed (see Note)
1-lb. can baby beets, drained
    and chopped
1¼ cups cherry tomatoes, halved
1 handful mint leaves

dressing
1 tablespoon apple cider
    vinegar or white wine
    vinegar
1 tablespoon olive oil

Put the beans, beets, and cherry tomatoes in a serving dish. Roughly chop half the mint leaves and mix them through the salad. Whisk the dressing ingredients in a small bowl and season to taste. Pour over the salad and mix gently. Sprinkle with the remaining mint leaves and serve.

Note: When available, use fresh cranberry beans (also known as borlotti beans) in this recipe. First blanch them in a pot of boiling water for several minutes until tender.

Serves 4 as a side salad

pork noodle salad

stock
1 cup chicken stock
3 cilantro roots
2 kaffir lime leaves
1¼ x 1¼-inch piece of fresh
    ginger, peeled and sliced

dressing
3 tablespoons lime juice
3 tablespoons fish sauce
1½ tablespoons brown sugar
¼ teaspoon ground white
    pepper

⅓ cup cloud ear mushrooms
3½ oz. dried rice vermicelli
1 small red chili, seeded
    and finely sliced, plus extra
    to serve
2 red Asian shallots, finely sliced
2 scallions, finely sliced
2 garlic cloves, crushed
9 oz. ground pork
1 handful cilantro leaves,
    chopped, plus extra whole
    leaves to serve
8 oak leaf lettuce leaves, torn
    or shredded
4 lime wedges

To make the stock, put the chicken stock, cilantro roots, lime leaves, and ginger in a saucepan with 1 cup water and bring to a boil. Reduce the heat and simmer for about 25 minutes or until reduced to 3/4 cup. Strain, return to the saucepan, and set aside.

Combine the dressing ingredients in a small bowl, stirring until the sugar has dissolved. Set aside until needed.

Discard the woody stems from the mushrooms, then thinly slice the caps. Soak the vermicelli in warm water for 5 minutes. Drain well, then cut into 1 1/4-inch lengths. Gently toss in a bowl with the mushrooms, chili, shallots, scallions, and garlic.

Return the stock to the heat and bring to a boil. Add the pork and stir, breaking up any lumps, for 1–2 minutes or until the pork changes color and is cooked through. Drain, then add to the vermicelli mixture with the dressing and chopped cilantro. Mix well, then season to taste.

Arrange the lettuce on a serving platter and spoon the pork mixture on top. Sprinkle with the extra chili slices and whole cilantro leaves and serve with the lime wedges.

Serves 4

cranberry bean, beet, and mint salad

smoked salmon and fennel salad

dressing
2 teaspoons Dijon mustard
1 teaspoon superfine sugar
1/2 cup olive oil
2 tablespoons lemon juice

2 fennel bulbs, thinly sliced,
    fronds reserved (see Note)
7 oz. smoked salmon, cut into
    strips
2 tablespoons snipped chives
arugula leaves, to serve
4 lemon wedges

Thoroughly whisk all the dressing ingredients together in a large bowl.

Chop enough reserved fennel fronds to fill a tablespoon and add to the dressing with the sliced fennel, smoked salmon, and chives. Season with salt and pepper and toss gently. Arrange some arugula leaves on four serving plates and pile the salad on top. Serve with the lemon wedges and some crusty bread.

Note: You could use a tablespoon of chopped fresh dill in place of the fennel fronds in this recipe.

Serves 4

Hawaiian poke salad

1/8 oz. dried wakame (seaweed)
1 lb. fish steaks, such as tuna
   or swordfish
1 large onion, finely chopped
6 scallions, finely sliced
2 small red chilies, cut
   into thin strips

4 tablespoons low-salt soy sauce
1 tablespoon sesame oil
4–6 lettuce leaves
1 tablespoon sesame seeds,
   toasted
4 lime wedges

Soak the wakame in a bowl of cold water for 15 minutes. Drain well.

Cut the fish into small cubes and place in a nonmetallic bowl with the wakame, onion, scallions, chilies, soy sauce, and sesame oil. Cover and refrigerate for 4 hours.

Line a serving platter with lettuce leaves. Top with the marinated fish and sprinkle with the toasted sesame seeds. Serve with lime wedges.

Serves 4

Studded with salty olives, crispy prosciutto, and cool sweet mint, every mouthful is a joy—a sensation in a bowl.

fennel and crispy prosciutto salad

sherry vinegar dressing	2 small fennel bulbs
2 tablespoons sherry vinegar	2 cucumbers
3 tablespoons olive oil	3/4 cup small whole black olives
	6 slices of prosciutto, chopped
	1 handful mint leaves

First, make the sherry vinegar dressing. Whisk the vinegar and oil in a small bowl and season with a little salt and black pepper. Set aside.

Next, prepare the fennel. Slice off and discard the feathery fronds and stalks from the top of the bulbs. Discard the outer layer from each fennel bulb, then cut a thin slice from the bottom of each bulb to form a flat base. Sit the fennel upright on a chopping board and slice it very thinly. Transfer the slices to a bowl and pour two thirds of the dressing over them. Toss well and allow to marinate for 2 hours, or up to 4 hours.

Slice the cucumbers in half lengthwise and scoop out the seeds using a spoon. Chop again at about $1/2$-inch intervals and put the cucumber slices in a serving dish with the olives.

Heat a frying pan over high heat. When the pan is hot, add the prosciutto and dry-fry until crispy, about 2 minutes. Remove from the pan, allow to cool a little, and cut into strips.

Add the fennel with all its marinade to the cucumber and olives. Pour over the remaining dressing and toss well. Top with the crispy prosciutto and mint leaves and serve.

Serves 4 as a side salad

fennel and crispy prosciutto salad

tropical sprout salad

1 small papaya
2 tablespoons lime juice
1/2 cup snow pea sprouts
2 small kiwifruit, peeled and thinly sliced
1/2 cup alfalfa sprouts

Peel the papaya, cut it in half, and scoop out the seeds. Cut the flesh into 1/2-inch slices and arrange in a single layer on a board or plate. Drizzle with the lime juice and set aside for 10 minutes.

Arrange half the papaya slices in a layer in a serving bowl, then half the snow pea sprouts, half the kiwifruit slices, and half the alfalfa sprouts. Repeat with the remaining ingredients and serve at once.

Serves 4 as a side salad

sun-dried tomato and baby spinach salad

1 preserved lemon quarter	1/3 cup small black olives
2 heaping cups baby spinach leaves	1 cup sun-dried tomatoes, sliced
	1 1/2 tablespoons lemon juice
3–4 marinated artichoke hearts, drained and quartered	2 tablespoons olive oil
	1 large garlic clove, crushed

Remove the flesh from the preserved lemon. Rinse the rind thoroughly under running water, then drain well and thinly slice it. Toss in a serving bowl with the spinach, artichokes, olives, and tomatoes.

Put the lemon juice, oil, and garlic in a small bowl. Season and mix well, then pour over the salad and toss to coat. Serve immediately.

Serves 4 as a side salad

Tender young spring vegetables are a gift of nature and are at their best in this delicate salad with its zesty dressing.

chicken and spring vegetable salad

1¹/₄ lb. boneless, skinless
  chicken breasts
¹/₂ lime, juiced
4 kaffir lime leaves, shredded
¹/₂ onion, peeled
6 black peppercorns
1 bunch asparagus
1¹/₄ cups fava beans, defrosted
  if frozen
2 cups baby green beans

lemon tarragon dressing
1 tablespoon olive oil
2 tablespoons lemon juice
2 tablespoons chopped
  tarragon leaves

Half-fill a large pot with water. Add the chicken, lime juice, lime leaves, onion, and peppercorns. Cover and bring slowly to a boil, then reduce the heat and simmer for 3 minutes. Turn off the heat and let the chicken cool in the broth for at least 30 minutes—it will continue to cook during this time.

Meanwhile, combine the lemon tarragon dressing ingredients in a small bowl. Season lightly with salt and pepper, mix well, and set aside.

Snap the woody ends off the asparagus and discard. Bring another pot of water to a boil and add a pinch of salt. Add the fava beans and cook for 1 minute, then add the green beans and simmer for 1 minute. Add the asparagus and cook for another minute. Drain well, refresh under cold water, and drain well again.

Slice the asparagus spears lengthwise and place them in a serving dish with the green beans. Remove the skins from the fava beans and add the beans to the serving dish.

Remove the cooled chicken from the poaching liquid. Shred the meat, then gently mix it into the salad with the dressing. Serve at once.

Serves 4

chicken and spring vegetable salad

Moroccan carrot salad with green olives and mint

harissa dressing
1 1/2 teaspoons cumin seeds
1/2 teaspoon coriander seeds
1 tablespoon red wine vinegar
2 tablespoons olive oil
1 garlic clove, crushed
2 teaspoons harissa
1/4 teaspoon orange
    flower water

1 1/4 lb. carrots, tops trimmed,
    well scrubbed
8 large green olives, pitted
    and finely sliced
2 tablespoons shredded mint
1 cup watercress leaves

To make the harissa dressing, dry-fry the cumin and coriander seeds in a small frying pan over medium heat for 30 seconds or until fragrant. Allow to cool, then grind with a mortar and pestle or spice grinder. Place in a large mixing bowl with the remaining dressing ingredients and whisk well.

Blanch the carrots in a pot of boiling salted water for 5 minutes or until almost tender. Drain into a colander and allow to dry for a few minutes. While the carrots are still hot, gently swirl them around in the harissa dressing until well coated. Allow to cool to room temperature.

Add the olives and mint to the infused carrots, season well, and toss gently to combine. Serve on a bed of watercress leaves.

Serves 4 as a side salad

cherry and pear tomato salad with white beans

3 tablespoons olive oil
2 red Asian shallots, finely diced
1 large garlic clove, crushed
1¹/2 tablespoons lemon juice
9-oz. carton cherry tomatoes, halved
9-oz. carton yellow pear tomatoes, halved
15-oz. can white beans, drained and rinsed
1 large handful basil leaves, roughly torn
2 tablespoons chopped parsley

Put the oil, shallots, garlic, and lemon juice in a small bowl and whisk well.

Put all the tomatoes in a serving bowl with the white beans. Drizzle with the shallot dressing and sprinkle the basil and parsley on top. Toss together gently and serve.

Serves 4 as a side dish

Here, charbroiled chicken gets a smoky, spicy edge, brightened with a lemony yogurt dressing for extra verve and pizzazz.

charbroiled chicken and sprout salad

1¼ lb. boneless, skinless chicken breasts
1 tablespoon olive oil
1 teaspoon ground cumin
1 teaspoon ground coriander
1 tablespoon lemon juice
1 head romaine lettuce, leaves roughly torn
½ cup snow pea sprouts, white ends trimmed

yogurt and caper dressing
1½ cups low-fat plain yogurt
2 tablespoons capers, rinsed, drained, and chopped
4 tablespoons lemon juice

Put the chicken breasts in a shallow, nonmetallic dish. In a small bowl, mix together the oil, cumin, coriander, and lemon juice. Pour the mixture all over the chicken, rubbing it in thoroughly to coat all sides. Cover and marinate in the fridge for 1 hour, or up to 8 hours.

Nearer to serving time, make the yogurt and caper dressing. Put all the ingredients in a small bowl and add a few grinds of black pepper and 1–2 tablespoons of water to thin it slightly. Whisk well and set aside.

Heat the grill or a charbroil pan to medium. Add the chicken and cook for 6–8 minutes on one side, then turn and cook for an additional 4 minutes or until cooked through. Remove from the heat and allow to cool slightly, then slice into strips.

Put the lettuce and snow pea sprouts in a serving dish and add the sliced chicken. Pour over the dressing, mix gently, and serve.

Serves 4

charbroiled chicken and sprout salad

snow pea salad with Japanese dressing

2 cups snow peas, trimmed
1/2 cup snow pea sprouts
1 small red bell pepper,
   julienned
2 teaspoons toasted
   sesame seeds

Japanese dressing
1/2 teaspoon dashi granules
1 tablespoon soy sauce

1 tablespoon mirin
1 teaspoon brown sugar
1 garlic clove, crushed
1 teaspoon finely chopped
   fresh ginger
1/4 teaspoon sesame oil
1 tablespoon vegetable oil
2 teaspoons toasted sesame
   seeds

Bring a pot of water to a boil, add the snow peas, and blanch for 1 minute. Drain and refresh under cold water, then drain again. Toss in a serving bowl with the snow pea sprouts and bell pepper.

To make the dressing, dissolve the dashi granules in 1 1/2 tablespoons of hot water. Pour into a small bowl, add the remaining dressing ingredients, and whisk well. Pour the dressing over the snow peas, toss well, and season to taste. Sprinkle with the sesame seeds and serve.

Serves 4 as a side salad

pear and sprout salad with sesame dressing

2 small firm, ripe pears
2 cups snow pea sprouts
2 cups bean sprouts, trimmed
1 small bunch chives, snipped
    into 1^1/$_2$-inch lengths
^{3}/$_4$ cup snow peas, julienned
1 celery stalk, julienned
1 small handful cilantro sprigs
1 teaspoon sesame seeds

sesame dressing
1^1/$_2$ tablespoons soy sauce
1 teaspoon sesame oil
1 tablespoon brown sugar
1^1/$_2$ tablespoons peanut oil
1 tablespoon rice vinegar

Peel and core the pears, then slice them into thin strips. Put the pear strips in a bowl and cover with water to prevent discoloration.

Put all the sesame dressing ingredients in a small screw-top jar and shake well to dissolve the sugar.

Drain the pears and put in a large serving bowl with the snow pea sprouts, bean sprouts, chives, snow peas, celery, and cilantro. Pour the dressing over, toss lightly, sprinkle with the sesame seeds, and serve.

Serves 4 as a side salad

Roasting draws the sweetness from the fennel and makes
a tender foil for sweet, juicy slivers of orange.

roasted fennel and orange salad

8 baby fennel bulbs
$1/3$ cup olive oil
2 oranges
1 tablespoon lemon juice
1 red onion, halved and thinly sliced
$1/2$ cup Kalamata olives
2 tablespoons roughly chopped mint
1 tablespoon roughly chopped Italian parsley

Preheat the oven to 400°F. Trim the fronds from the fennel and reserve.
Remove the stalks and cut a $1/4$-inch slice off the base of each fennel bulb.
Slice each bulb into six wedges and arrange in a baking dish. Drizzle with
3 tablespoons of the oil and season well. Bake for 40–45 minutes or until
tender and slightly caramelized, turning once or twice during cooking.
Allow to cool.

Cut a thin slice off the top and bottom of each orange. Using a sharp knife, slice off the skin and pith, removing as much of the bitter white pith as possible. Slice down the side of a segment between the flesh and the membrane (do this over a bowl to catch the juices). Repeat with the other side and lift the segment out. Remove all the segments from both oranges in the same way, squeezing out any juice remaining in the membranes.

Add the lemon juice to the juice caught from the oranges and whisk in the remaining oil until emulsified. Season well. Put the orange segments, onion, and olives in a bowl, pour on half the dressing, and add half the mint. Mix well, then transfer to a serving dish. Top with the fennel, drizzle with the remaining dressing, and sprinkle with the parsley and remaining mint. Chop the reserved fennel fronds, sprinkle over the salad, and serve.

Serves 4 as a side salad

snow pea salad with Japanese dressing

lunch box   Hasty lunches are the downfall of many a dedicated dieter, health nut, or office gourmand, and yet organizing a packed lunch can seem all too daunting in the cold light of morning. Not anymore. Here's all the inspiration you need to plan ahead a little and pack a pretty lunch with a super energy-giving salad to power you through the day.

Being aware of what we eat is not just about watching our weight. For many of us it is simply about aspiring to an optimal state of health and well-being. Evaluating the quality of the food we consume is a simple way to stay on top and, by and large, most of us manage to do pretty well, except for the daily downfall—lunch on the run. If you're in the habit of buying lunch, whether from a food court, deli, or fast-food joint, it can be hard to know what you are really consuming. And while school days may have ruined your appetite for packed lunches, it's time to relinquish those musty memories of soggy sandwiches and browning bananas. Variety, sustenance, and balance are easy to achieve on a daily basis when you explore the range of delicious salads that are perfect for packing up and taking with you. It's so simple to create inspiring and healthy lunches: all the recipes in this chapter can be made ahead and packed the night before, ready to pop in your bag as you're dashing out the door. Even better, there's enough for two helpings, so pack another lunch for a loved one, or save it for the following day. And when it comes to stashing your salad, you can always resort to the ever-sensible resealable plastic container, or you could really have some fun and break up the humdrum routine. Noodle boxes and kitsch creations are just a couple of ideas to dress it all up. Take-out chopsticks and funky napkins are a cute way to treat yourself as you would someone else—like you are special and deserve the extra treatment. Now there's something to look forward to in the middle of the workaday day!

Asian tofu salad

1/2 red bell pepper
1/2 green bell pepper
2/3 cup bean sprouts, trimmed
2 scallions, sliced
1 tablespoon chopped cilantro
3 cups shredded Chinese
   cabbage
11/2 tablespoons chopped
   roasted peanuts
7 oz. firm tofu
11/2 tablespoons peanut oil

dressing
1 tablespoon sweet chili sauce
1 tablespoon lime juice
1/4 teaspoon sesame oil
1 tablespoon light soy sauce
1 garlic clove, finely chopped
11/2 teaspoons finely grated
   fresh ginger
11/2 tablespoons peanut oil

Thinly slice the red and green bell pepper and toss in a large bowl with the bean sprouts, scallions, cilantro, cabbage, and peanuts.

Cut the tofu into 31/4 x 3/4-inch slices. Heat the oil in a large frying pan and cook the tofu over medium heat for 2–3 minutes on each side or until golden with a crispy edge. Add the tofu to the salad.

To make the dressing, whisk all the ingredients in a small bowl until well combined. Toss through the salad and divide between two resealable containers.

Makes 2 salads

Asian pork salad

ginger and chili dressing
1¼-inch piece of fresh ginger, peeled and julienned
1 teaspoon rice vinegar
½ small red chili, seeded and finely chopped
1 tablespoon light soy sauce
a few drops of sesame oil
½ star anise
1 teaspoon lime juice

4½ oz. Chinese roast pork (char sui)
½ cup snow pea sprouts
2 scallions, thinly sliced diagonally
½ small red bell pepper, thinly sliced

To make the ginger and chili dressing, combine the ginger, vinegar, chili, soy sauce, sesame oil, star anise, and lime juice in a small saucepan. Gently warm for 2 minutes or until just about to come to a boil, then set aside to cool. Once it has cooled, remove the star anise.

Thinly slice the pork and divide between two resealable containers along with the snow pea sprouts, scallions, and bell pepper. Pack the dressing separately and drizzle over the salad just before eating.

Makes 2 salads

Wild rice has a tough shell but a tender heart. Its nutty flavor brings a satisfying bite to this surprisingly feisty salad.

Chinese roast chicken with wild rice

1/4 cup wild rice
1/4 cup jasmine rice
1/2 small Chinese roast chicken
1 tablespoon chopped mint
1 tablespoon chopped cilantro
1/2 cucumber
2 scallions, sliced diagonally
1 tablespoon roasted unsalted
    peanuts, roughly chopped
sweet chili sauce, to serve

mirin dressing
2 teaspoons mirin
1 teaspoon Chinese rice wine
1/2 teaspoon soy sauce
1/2 teaspoon lime juice
1 teaspoon sweet chili sauce

Bring a large pot of water to a boil and add the wild rice and 1 teaspoon of salt. Cook for 30 minutes, then add the jasmine rice and cook for an additional 10 minutes or until both rices are tender. Drain the rice, rinse under cold water, and drain again.

Shred the chicken (including the skin) into bite-size pieces and put in a large bowl. Add the mint and cilantro. Cut the cucumber through the center (do not peel) and thinly slice it diagonally. Add to the chicken with the rice, scallions, and peanuts.

Mix together all the mirin dressing ingredients in a small bowl, pour over the salad, and toss to combine. Divide between two resealable containers and drizzle with a little sweet chili sauce.

Makes 2 salads

Asian pork salad

farfalle salad with sun-dried tomatoes and spinach

2 cups farfalle or spiral pasta
1 scallion, finely sliced
   diagonally
3 sun-dried tomatoes, cut
   into strips
4 cups spinach, stalks trimmed
   and leaves shredded
1 tablespoon toasted pine nuts
1 teaspoon chopped oregano

dressing
1 tablespoon olive oil
1/4 teaspoon chopped chili
1 small garlic clove, crushed

Cook the pasta in a large pot of boiling salted water until al dente. Drain, rinse under cold water, and drain again. Allow the pasta to cool, then transfer to a large bowl. Add the scallion, tomatoes, spinach, pine nuts, and oregano.

Put all the dressing ingredients in a small screw-top jar and season with salt and pepper. Shake well and pour all over the salad. Gently toss together and divide between two resealable containers.

Makes 2 salads

haloumi and asparagus salad with salsa verde

salsa verde
1 small handful basil leaves
1 small handful mint leaves
1 large handful parsley leaves
1 tablespoon baby capers,
    rinsed and drained
1 garlic clove
1 tablespoon olive oil

1/2 tablespoon lemon juice
1/2 tablespoon lime juice

4 1/2 oz. haloumi cheese
1 bunch thin asparagus spears
1 tablespoon garlic oil or olive oil
1 cup mixed salad leaves

To make the salsa verde, blend the herbs, capers, garlic, and oil in a food processor until smooth. Add the lemon and lime juice, and pulse briefly.

Heat a charbroil pan to medium. Cut the haloumi into 1/2-inch slices, then cut each slice into two small triangles. Brush the haloumi and asparagus with the garlic oil. Charbroil the asparagus for 1 minute or until just tender, then charbroil the haloumi for about 45 seconds on each side, or until grill marks appear.

Divide the salad leaves between two resealable containers and top with the haloumi and asparagus. Pack the salsa verde separately and drizzle over the salad just before eating.

Makes 2 salads

Crispy apple, peppery arugula, and smoky chicken: this snappy salad will pick you up in a flash.

smoked chicken and pasta salad with mustard dressing

4 oz. bucatini pasta (see Note)
9 oz. smoked chicken breast
1 small Fuji apple
4 small radishes, thinly sliced
2 scallions, finely sliced
1/2 small bunch arugula, trimmed

mustard dressing
1/2 tablespoon balsamic vinegar
3 1/2 tablespoons olive oil
1/2 tablespoon lemon juice
1 1/2 tablespoons whole-grain mustard

Cook the pasta in a large pot of boiling salted water until al dente. Drain, rinse under cold water, and drain again. Place in a large bowl.

Put all the mustard dressing ingredients in a screw-top jar and shake well. Season to taste with salt and freshly cracked pepper. Toss one third of the dressing through the pasta and set aside for 30 minutes.

Cut the chicken breast into strips on the diagonal and place in a bowl. Leaving the skin on the apple, cut it into quarters, then core the quarters and cut them into cubes. Add them to the chicken with the radishes, scallions, and arugula. Pour over the remaining dressing and toss lightly.

Gently toss the chicken mixture through the pasta until well combined. Divide between two resealable containers and enjoy with fresh, crusty bread.

Note: Bucatini is a thick, spaghetti-like pasta with a hollow center and a chewy texture.

Makes 2 salads

haloumi and asparagus salad with salsa verde

avocado, bacon, and tomato salad

3 garlic cloves, unpeeled
2 tablespoons olive oil
1 tablespoon balsamic vinegar
1 teaspoon Dijon mustard
4 1/2 oz. rindless smoked
   Canadian bacon (see Note)
   or bacon slices

1 cup green salad leaves
1/2 small red onion, finely sliced
1 avocado, cut into chunks
2 small firm, ripe tomatoes,
   cut into chunks

Preheat the oven to 350°F. Place the unpeeled garlic cloves on a baking sheet and roast for 30 minutes. Remove, allow to cool, then squeeze the flesh out of the skins and mash in a small bowl. Add the oil, vinegar, and mustard, whisk well to make a dressing, and season to taste.

Chop the bacon into bite-size pieces, then cook under a medium-hot broiler or in a frying pan over medium heat for 3–5 minutes or until crisp. Divide between two resealable containers with the salad leaves, onion, avocado, and tomato. Gently toss together. Pack the dressing separately and, just before eating, give it a good shake and drizzle over the salad.

Note: Smoked Canadian bacon is available from most delicatessens. If you can't find it, you can use bacon slices instead.

Makes 2 salads

chili chicken and cashew salad

2 teaspoons olive oil
10 1/2 oz. boneless, skinless
   chicken breasts
1 cup salad leaves
1 cup cherry tomatoes, halved
1/2 cucumber, cut into
   bite-size chunks
1/2 cup snow pea sprouts,
   trimmed
1/4 cup cashews, roughly
   chopped

dressing
1 1/2 tablespoons sweet
   chili sauce
1 tablespoon lime juice
1 teaspoon fish sauce
1 tablespoon chopped cilantro
1 small garlic clove, crushed
1/2 small red chili, finely chopped
1 teaspoon grated fresh ginger
2 teaspoons peanut or
   sesame oil

Heat the oil in a frying pan or charbroil pan. Add the chicken and cook over medium heat for 5–8 minutes on each side or until cooked through. While still hot, slice each breast widthwise into strips.

Combine the dressing ingredients in a large bowl and mix well. Toss the warm chicken strips through the dressing and allow to cool slightly. Divide the salad leaves, tomatoes, cucumber, and snow pea sprouts between two resealable containers and sprinkle with the cashews. Pack the dressed chicken separately and mix through the salad just before eating.

Makes 2 salads

Marinating chicken makes it exquisitely tender and allows all the dusky, musky spices to permeate deep into the meat.

Indian marinated chicken salad

1¹/2 tablespoons lemon juice
1 teaspoon garam masala
¹/2 teaspoon ground turmeric
2 teaspoons finely grated
    fresh ginger
1 garlic clove, finely chopped
1¹/2 tablespoons vegetable oil
11 oz. boneless, skinless chicken
    breasts
¹/2 onion, thinly sliced
1 zucchini, thinly sliced
    diagonally

2 cups watercress leaves
¹/2 cup freshly podded peas
1 tomato, finely chopped
1 small handful cilantro leaves

yogurt dressing

¹/2 teaspoon cumin seeds
¹/4 teaspoon coriander seeds
2 tablespoons plain yogurt
1 tablespoon chopped mint
1 tablespoon lemon juice

Combine the lemon juice, garam masala, turmeric, ginger, garlic, and 1 teaspoon of the oil in a large bowl. Add the chicken and onion, toss well to coat all over, then cover and refrigerate for 1 hour.

Remove the onion from the chicken marinade, then heat 1 tablespoon of the oil in a large frying pan. Cook the chicken over medium heat for about 4–5 minutes on each side or until cooked through. Remove the chicken from the pan and let stand for 5 minutes. Cut each breast across the grain into 1/2-inch slices.

Heat the remaining oil in the pan and sauté the zucchini and marinated onion for 2 minutes or until lightly golden and tender. Toss in a large bowl with the watercress. Cook the peas in boiling water for 5 minutes or until tender, then drain and rinse under cold water to cool. Add to the salad with the chicken, tomato, and cilantro.

To make the yogurt dressing, dry-fry the cumin and coriander seeds in a frying pan over medium heat for 1–2 minutes or until fragrant. Put the seeds in a mortar (or spice grinder) and pound them to a powder. Mix together with the yogurt, mint, and lemon juice. Gently fold the dressing through the salad and divide between two resealable containers.

Makes 2 salads

chili chicken and
cashew salad

tomato and bocconcini salad

basil oil
1/2 cup olive oil
1 large handful basil
    leaves, torn
1 tablespoon balsamic vinegar

3 plum tomatoes, halved
6 oz. cherry bocconcini or baby
    mozzarella cheese
1 1/2 cups mizuna lettuce leaves
    or baby arugula leaves

To make the basil oil, put the oil and basil leaves in a saucepan. Stir gently over medium heat for 3–5 minutes or until very hot but not smoking. Remove from the heat and discard the basil. Reserve 1 tablespoon of the basil oil and mix it with the vinegar; store the remainder in a clean jar in the refrigerator to use in salad dressings and pasta sauces.

Arrange the tomato, bocconcini, and lettuce in two resealable containers. Drizzle with the basil oil and sprinkle with sea salt and cracked black pepper.

Makes 2 salads

caramelized onion and potato salad

1 tablespoon olive oil
3 red onions, thinly sliced
10 small fingerling or new
    potatoes, unpeeled
2 slices of bacon, rind removed
1/2 bunch chives, snipped

lemon mayonnaise
1/2 cup mayonnaise
2 teaspoons Dijon mustard
1/2 lemon, juiced
1 tablespoon sour cream

Heat the oil in a large, heavy-based frying pan. Add the onion and cook, stirring, over low heat for 40 minutes or until soft and caramelized.

Cut any large potatoes into chunks (leave the small ones whole). Cook in boiling water for 10 minutes or until just tender, then drain. Place in a large bowl with the onion and most of the chives and mix well.

Meanwhile, broil the bacon until crisp. Drain on crumpled paper towels and allow to cool slightly, then chop coarsely.

Whisk together the lemon mayonnaise ingredients, pour over the salad, and toss to coat. Divide between two resealable containers and sprinkle with the bacon and reserved chives.

Makes 2 salads

The classic clash of sweet and sour is a delectable match for tender pork, jazzed up with sweet pineapple and crunchy nuts.

sweet and sour pork salad

marinade
1 tablespoon soy sauce
2 teaspoons honey
2 teaspoons dry sherry

9 oz. pork tenderloin, trimmed
1 tablespoon peanut oil
1¹/₂ cups finely shredded
   Chinese cabbage

1 small carrot, grated
2 scallions, finely sliced on
   the diagonal
8-oz. can pineapple pieces,
   drained (reserve 1 tablespoon
   of the juice)
1 tablespoon white wine
   vinegar
¹/₄ teaspoon brown sugar

Put all the marinade ingredients in a small screw-top jar and shake well.

Place the pork tenderloin in a bowl and pour over the marinade. Turn to coat all sides, then cover with plastic wrap and refrigerate for at least 2 hours—or preferably overnight—turning occasionally.

Heat half the oil in a heavy-based pan. Add the pork tenderloin and cook over medium heat for 10 minutes, turning to brown all sides. Remove to a plate and cover loosely with foil. Allow to cool, then slice.

Toss the cabbage, carrot, scallions, and pineapple together in a large bowl. Put the reserved pineapple juice in a small screw-top jar with the remaining oil, vinegar, and sugar and shake well. Pour the dressing over the salad and toss gently to combine. Divide between two resealable containers and top with the sliced pork.

Makes 2 salads

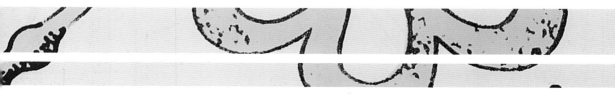

tomato and bocconcini salad

Tuscan bread salad

3 thick slices of Italian bread,
   crusts removed
2 large vine-ripened tomatoes
1½ tablespoons olive oil
1 teaspoon lemon juice
2 teaspoons red wine vinegar

2 anchovy fillets, finely chopped
1 teaspoon baby capers, rinsed,
   drained, and finely chopped
1 garlic clove, crushed
1 handful basil leaves

Preheat the oven to 425°F. Tear the bread into 3/4-inch chunks, then spread on a baking sheet and bake for 5–7 minutes or until golden. Cool on a wire rack.

Score a cross in the base of each tomato. Place in a heatproof bowl and cover with boiling water. Leave for 30 seconds, then plunge in cold water and peel the skin from the cross. Cut a tomato in half and squeeze the juice and seeds into a bowl; chop and reserve the flesh. Add the oil, lemon juice, vinegar, anchovies, capers, and garlic to the tomato juice, and season.

Seed and slice the remaining tomato and place in a large bowl with the reserved chopped tomato flesh and most of the basil. Add the dressing and toasted bread and toss. Divide between two resealable containers, sprinkle with the remaining basil, then season. Serve at room temperature.

Makes 2 salads

herbed feta salad

1 small slice thick white bread,
    crust removed
2$1/2$ oz. feta cheese, cubed
$1/4$ red-leaf lettuce, leaves torn
$1/4$ butter, coral, or oak leaf
    lettuce, leaves torn

dressing
1 small garlic clove, crushed
1 heaping teaspoon finely
    chopped marjoram
1 heaping teaspoon finely
    snipped chives
1 heaping teaspoon finely
    chopped basil
1 tablespoon white wine vinegar
1$1/2$ tablespoons olive oil

Preheat the oven to 350°F. Cut the bread into cubes and spread on a baking sheet. Bake for 10 minutes or until crisp and lightly golden. Put the baking sheet on a rack and allow to cool completely.

Put the feta in a bowl. Combine all the dressing ingredients in a small screw-top jar and shake for 30 seconds. Pour over the feta, cover with plastic wrap, and marinate in the refrigerator, stirring occasionally.

While the cheese is marinating, divide the lettuce leaves and bread cubes between two resealable containers. Pack the dressed feta separately and mix it into the salad just before eating.

Makes 2 salads

There's no nicer way to use up leftover chicken than this tasty salad studded with plump golden raisins and creamy cashews.

chicken with mixed rice, golden raisins, and cashews

$2/3$ cup mixed rice blend
   (see Note)
$1/3$ cup cashews
1 cup shredded roasted
   or grilled chicken
$1/3$ cup golden raisins
8–10 cilantro sprigs

cilantro dressing
2 tablespoons olive oil
1 tablespoon red wine vinegar
1 teaspoon whole-grain mustard
2 tablespoons finely chopped
   cilantro leaves

Cook the rice according to the package instructions, then drain well. Rinse under cold water and drain well again. Fluff up with a fork to separate the grains, then allow to cool in a sieve over a saucepan.

While the rice is cooling, put a frying pan over high heat. Add the cashews and dry-fry for 1–2 minutes, tossing them so they color evenly. When the nuts are lightly toasted, put them on a chopping board, allow to cool, then roughly chop them.

Put all the cilantro dressing ingredients except the cilantro leaves in a small bowl and whisk until well combined. Season lightly with salt and black pepper, then stir in the cilantro.

When the rice is cold, mix in the shredded chicken, cashews, and golden raisins. Stir in the dressing, season with salt and pepper, and mix well. Divide between two resealable containers and sprinkle with cilantro sprigs.

Note: You could also use leftover rice for this recipe. You will need about 2 cups of cold cooked rice.

Makes 2 salads

chicken with mixed rice, golden raisins, and cashews

minty lentil salad

½ cup brown lentils
½ chicken or vegetable stock
  cube, crumbled
1 tomato, cut into ½-inch
  cubes
2 scallions, sliced

mint dressing
1 tablespoon vegetable oil
1 teaspoon apple cider vinegar
2 teaspoons chopped mint
¼ teaspoon ground cumin
pinch of cayenne pepper

Put the lentils in a pot, cover with cold water, and add the stock cube. Bring to a boil, then reduce the heat and simmer for 20 minutes or until the lentils are tender—don't overcook or the lentils will become mushy. Drain and set aside to cool.

Gently toss the lentils in a bowl with the tomato and scallions. Put the mint dressing ingredients in a small screw-top jar and shake well. Drizzle the dressing over the salad, toss gently to combine, then divide between two resealable containers. Serve with fresh, crusty bread.

Makes 2 salads

beet and chive salad

12 baby beets
2 tablespoons pine nuts or
   pistachios
1 cup watercress leaves
1 tablespoon snipped chives

dressing
$1/4$ teaspoon honey
$1/4$ teaspoon Dijon mustard
1 tablespoon balsamic vinegar
$1^1/_2$ tablespoons olive oil

Preheat the oven to 400°F. Trim the beet bulbs and scrub them well. Put them in a roasting dish, cover with foil, and roast for 1 hour or until tender. Remove from the oven and allow to cool.

Turn the oven down to 350°F. Spread the nuts on a baking sheet and bake for 5 minutes or until lightly golden, ensuring they don't burn. Remove from the oven, allow to cool, then roughly chop.

To make the dressing, combine the honey, mustard, and vinegar in a small bowl. Whisk in the oil with a fork until well combined, then season to taste.

Peel the beets, wearing gloves, and halve any larger ones. Divide between two resealable containers with the watercress and chives, and sprinkle with the nuts. Pack the dressing separately and drizzle over the salad just before eating.

Makes 2 salads

Beets burst with sweet, mellow flavor, and here their scarlet juices mingle with creamy white goat cheese.

fresh beet and goat cheese salad

2 beets, with leaves
1 cup green beans, trimmed
2 oz. goat cheese

caper dressing
2 teaspoons red wine vinegar
1 tablespoon extra-virgin olive oil
1 garlic clove, crushed
2 teaspoons capers, rinsed, drained, and coarsely chopped

Trim the leaves from the beets. Scrub the bulbs and wash the leaves well. Bring a large pot of water to a boil, add the beets, then reduce the heat and simmer, covered, for about 30 minutes or until tender. Drain and allow to cool. Wearing gloves to protect your hands from staining, peel the skins off the beets and cut the bulbs into wedges.

Meanwhile, bring a pot of lightly salted water to a boil, add the beans, and blanch until bright green and just tender, about 2–3 minutes. Remove with tongs and plunge into a bowl of cold water. Drain well.

Add the beet leaves to the pot of boiling water and cook for about 3–5 minutes or until the leaves and stems are tender. Drain, plunge into a bowl of cold water, then drain well again.

To make the caper dressing, put the vinegar, oil, garlic, and capers in a small screw-top jar with $1/4$ teaspoon each of salt and cracked black pepper. Shake vigorously until well combined.

Divide the beans, beets, and beet leaves between two resealable containers. Crumble the goat cheese on top and drizzle with the dressing.

Makes 2 salads

beet and chive salad

egg salad with dill mayonnaise

dill mayonnaise
1 egg yolk
1 tablespoon lemon juice
2 teaspoons Dijon mustard
1/4 cup olive oil
1/4 cup safflower oil
2 tablespoons chopped dill

2 tablespoons crème fraîche
   or sour cream
2 tablespoons baby capers,
   rinsed and drained

5 large hard-boiled eggs, peeled
2/3 cup watercress

To make the dill mayonnaise, put the egg yolk, lemon juice, and mustard in a food processor or blender and season with salt and pepper. With the motor running, slowly add the combined olive oil and safflower oil, drop by drop at first, then slowly increasing the amount to a thin, steady stream as the mixture thickens. When all the oil has been added, put the mayonnaise in a bowl and gently stir in the dill, crème fraîche, and capers. This mayonnaise makes enough for more than one use, so transfer half the mayonnaise to a clean container and refrigerate for use in another salad.

Roughly chop the eggs and fold into the remaining mayonnaise, then divide between two resealable containers. Cut the green tips from the watercress and sprinkle them over the salad. Serve with fresh, crusty bread.

Makes 2 salads

charbroiled vegetable salad with balsamic dressing

2 baby eggplants
2 large plum tomatoes
1 red bell pepper
1/2 green bell pepper
1 zucchini
2 1/2 tablespoons olive oil
6 bocconcini or 12 small, fresh
    mozzarella cheeses

12 Ligurian or Kalamata olives
1 garlic clove, finely chopped
1 heaping teaspoon baby
    capers, rinsed and drained
1/4 teaspoon sugar
1 tablespoon balsamic vinegar

Cut the eggplants and tomatoes into quarters. Cut the bell peppers in half lengthwise, remove the seeds and membrane, then cut each half into thick strips. Thinly slice the zucchini on the diagonal.

Preheat a charbroil pan or the grill to high. Brush with 1/2 tablespoon of the oil and cook the vegetables in batches for about 2–3 minutes or until golden and slightly charred, adding a little more oil as needed. (The tomatoes are best cooked cut side down first.)

Put the vegetables and cheese in a large bowl. Mix together the olives, garlic, capers, sugar, and vinegar with the remaining oil, then pour over the salad and toss. Divide between two resealable containers and sprinkle with pepper.

Makes 2 salads

Fresh and wholesome, this cool, crunchy salad has a wicked streak—a sprinkling of incredibly addictive garlic croutons.

snow pea salad

garlic croutons
1½ slices thick white bread,
  crusts removed
3 tablespoons olive oil
1 small garlic clove, crushed

dressing
1 tablespoon olive oil
2 teaspoons mayonnaise
2 teaspoons sour cream
1 tablespoon lemon juice
½ teaspoon brown sugar

1 cup snow peas, trimmed and
  sliced diagonally
½ red bell pepper, sliced
1 cup cherry tomatoes
1 cup watercress sprigs
2 oak leaf lettuce leaves, torn
2 green-leaf lettuce leaves, torn
shaved Parmesan cheese,
  to serve

To make the garlic croutons, cut the bread into $^1/_2$-inch cubes. Heat the oil in a small, heavy-based frying pan and add the garlic. Stir in the bread cubes and cook over medium heat for about 4–5 minutes or until golden and crisp. Remove from the pan and drain thoroughly on crumpled paper towels.

Whisk all the dressing ingredients in a small bowl with some cracked black pepper for 2 minutes or until well combined.

Divide the snow peas, bell pepper, tomatoes, watercress, and lettuce leaves between two resealable containers. Sprinkle some Parmesan on top. Pack the croutons in a separate container so they stay crisp, and take the dressing in a separate container so the lettuce doesn't get soggy. Just before eating, drizzle the dressing over the salad and sprinkle with the croutons.

Makes 2 salads

charbroiled vegetable salad with
balsamic dressing

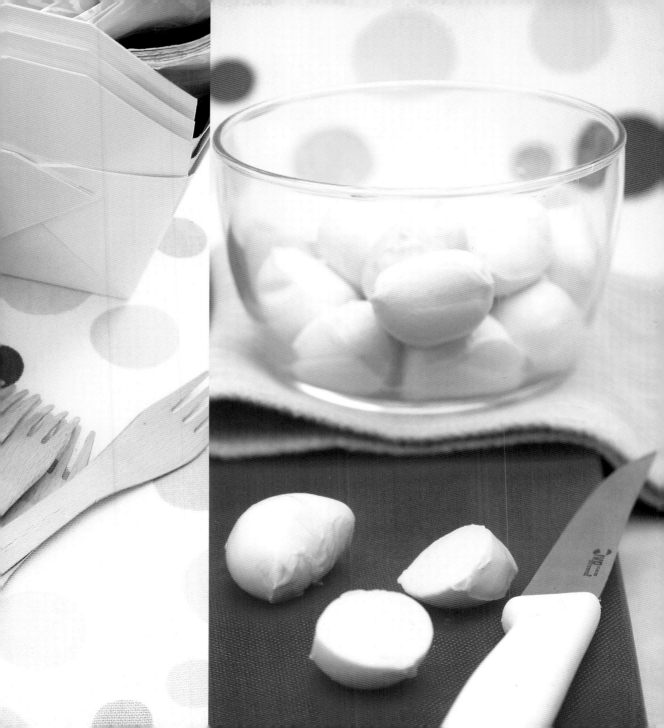

Vietnamese salad with lemongrass dressing

4 oz. dried rice vermicelli
1 small handful Vietnamese
   mint leaves, torn
1 small handful cilantro leaves
1/2 small red onion, thinly sliced
1 small green mango, peeled
   and julienned
1/2 cucumber, halved and
   thinly sliced
1/2 cup crushed peanuts

lemongrass dressing
3 tablespoons lime juice
2 teaspoons brown sugar
1 1/2 tablespoons seasoned
   rice vinegar
1 stem lemongrass, white part
   only, finely chopped
1 red chili, seeded and finely
   chopped
1 kaffir lime leaf, shredded

Put the noodles in a bowl, cover with boiling water, and soak for 10 minutes or until soft. Drain, rinse under cold water, and cut into short lengths. Toss in a large bowl with the mint, cilantro, onion, mango, cucumber, and three quarters of the peanuts, then divide between two resealable containers.

Whisk the dressing ingredients together and toss through the salad. Pack the remaining nuts separately and sprinkle over the salad just before eating.

Makes 2 salads

cottage cheese salad

1/2 sheet cracker bread
1 teaspoon canola oil
pinch of mild paprika
1 tablespoon snipped chives
1 cup cottage cheese

8 red oak leaf lettuce leaves
1/2 cup red grapes
1 small carrot, grated
2 tablespoons alfalfa sprouts

Preheat the oven to 350°F. Brush the cracker bread with the oil, sprinkle lightly with paprika, and cut into eight strips. Spread on a baking sheet and bake for 5 minutes or until golden. Allow to cool on a rack.

Mix the chives into the cottage cheese. Divide the lettuce, grapes, and carrot between two resealable containers, then arrange the cottage cheese and sprouts on top. Pack the cracker bread crisps separately so they don't become soggy, and eat them with the salad.

Makes 2 salads

Tender vegetables smothered in an irresistible satay dressing: this Indonesian classic will send your taste buds spinning!

gado gado

1 small carrot, thinly sliced
1/2 cup small cauliflower florets
6–8 snow peas, trimmed
heaping 1/2 cup bean sprouts,
    trimmed
4 well-shaped iceberg
    lettuce leaves
2 small potatoes, cooked and
    cut into thin slices
1/2 cucumber, thinly sliced
1 hard-boiled egg, peeled and
    cut into quarters
1 tomato, cut into wedges

peanut sauce
2 teaspoons vegetable oil
1/2 small onion, finely chopped
3 tablespoons crunchy
    peanut butter
1/3 cup coconut milk
1/2 teaspoon sambal oelek
2 teaspoons lemon juice
2 teaspoons kecap manis

Steam the carrot and cauliflower in a pot of boiling water for 5 minutes or until nearly tender. Add the snow peas and cook for 2 minutes. Add the bean sprouts and cook for 1 minute more; set aside and allow to cool.

To make the peanut sauce, heat the oil in a saucepan and sauté the onion over low heat for 5 minutes or until soft and lightly golden. Add the peanut butter, coconut milk, sambal oelek, lemon juice, kecap manis, and 3 tablespoons water, and stir well. Bring to a boil, stirring constantly, then reduce the heat and simmer for 5 minutes or until the sauce has reduced and thickened. Remove from the heat.

Sit one lettuce leaf inside another to form a lettuce cup. Make another lettuce cup in the same way and put them in two resealable containers. Arrange half the potato, carrot, cauliflower, snow peas, bean sprouts, and cucumber in each lettuce cup, then top with the egg and tomato. Pack the peanut sauce separately and drizzle over the salad just before eating.

Makes 2 salads

Vietnamese salad with lemongrass dressing

bulgur, feta, and parsley salad

1/2 cup bulgur wheat
2 tablespoons chopped
   Italian parsley
2 tablespoons chopped mint
4 scallions, finely chopped
2 firm, ripe tomatoes, halved,
   seeded, and diced

1 cucumber, halved,
   seeded, and diced
4 oz. feta cheese, crumbled
2 tablespoons lemon juice
2 tablespoons olive oil

Put the bulgur in a large bowl and add enough hot water to cover. Allow to soak for 15–20 minutes or until tender. Drain well, then thoroughly squeeze out all the excess liquid.

Gently toss the bulgur in a bowl with all the remaining ingredients. Season with sea salt and freshly ground black pepper and mix together well. Divide between two resealable containers and allow all the flavors to mingle for at least an hour.

Makes 2 salads

frisée salad with pancetta and toasts

vinaigrette
1/2 French shallot, finely
  chopped
2 teaspoons Dijon mustard
1 1/2 tablespoons tarragon
  vinegar
4 tablespoons extra-virgin
  olive oil

2 teaspoons olive oil
4 1/2 oz. pancetta, cut
  into fine strips
1/4 French baguette, sliced
2 garlic cloves
1/2 baby frisée, washed
  and dried
1/2 cup toasted walnuts

To make the vinaigrette, whisk the shallot, mustard, and vinegar in a small bowl. Slowly add the oil, whisking constantly until thickened. Set aside.

Heat the olive oil in a large frying pan. Add the pancetta, bread slices, and whole garlic cloves and cook over medium heat for 5–8 minutes or until the bread and pancetta are both crisp. Discard the garlic.

Arrange the pancetta in two resealable containers with the frisée and walnuts. Pack the toasted bread slices separately so they stay crisp and carry the vinaigrette separately so the lettuce doesn't become soggy. Just before eating, drizzle the vinaigrette over the salad and add the toasts.

Makes 2 salads

Couscous is the ultimate flavor absorber, soaking up the
aromatic dressing and making a fluffy base for nuts and veggies.

couscous salad

1/4 cup shelled pistachios
1 large wedge peeled kabocha
   squash, thinly sliced
1 zucchini, sliced
1 1/2 tablespoons olive oil
1/2 red bell pepper
1 cup instant couscous
11-oz. can chickpeas, drained
   and rinsed
2 scallions, sliced
1 handful mint, shredded

dressing
1 teaspoon cumin seeds
1 garlic clove, finely chopped
1 small red chili, seeded and
   finely chopped
1/2 cup chicken or vegetable
   stock
2 fresh bay leaves, torn
2 tablespoons lemon juice
3 tablespoons extra-virgin
   olive oil

Preheat the oven to 350°F. Spread the pistachios on a baking sheet and
bake for 5–10 minutes or until lightly golden—keep an eye on them, as
they burn easily. Remove from the oven, allow to cool, then roughly chop.

Drizzle the squash and zucchini with 1 tablespoon of the oil. Cook under a hot broiler for 4–5 minutes on each side or until golden.

Cut the bell pepper into large flat pieces and remove the seeds and membranes. Cook, skin side up, under the hot broiler until the skin blackens and blisters. Allow to cool in a plastic bag, then peel away the skin and cut the flesh into 1/2-inch strips.

Put the couscous in a large bowl. Cover with 1 cup boiling water, add the remaining oil, and stir gently. Cover with plastic wrap and let stand for 5 minutes. Fluff up the couscous with a fork, raking out any lumps, then add the pistachios, squash, zucchini, bell pepper, chickpeas, scallions, and mint. Toss well.

To make the dressing, gently dry-fry the cumin seeds in a heavy-based frying pan for 1–2 minutes or until fragrant. Pound to a powder with a mortar and pestle, then place in a bowl and mix in the garlic and chili.

Boil the stock in a saucepan with the bay leaves for 2 minutes or until reduced to 2 tablespoons of liquid. Strain the stock into the spice mixture and discard the bay leaves. Add the lemon juice, then whisk in the oil with a fork. Season to taste, then gently toss through the couscous and divide between two resealable containers.

Makes 2 salads

bulgur, feta, and parsley salad

crunchy rice salad

1/2 cup basmati or jasmine rice
1 carrot, sliced diagonally
1/2 green bell pepper, julienned
2/3 cup baby corn, cut into
   3/4-inch lengths
1 scallion, sliced
3 oz. Chinese roast pork
   (char siu), thinly sliced

dressing
1 tablespoon peanut oil
2 teaspoons sesame oil
1 teaspoon lime juice
1 teaspoon soy sauce

Cook the rice in a large pot of boiling water until just tender. Drain, rinse under cold water, and drain again thoroughly. Spread over a plate and allow to cool. When the rice has cooled, toss it in a bowl with the carrot, bell pepper, corn, scallion, and pork.

Put the dressing ingredients in a small screw-top jar and shake well. Pour over the salad and toss well, then divide between two resealable containers.

Makes 2 salads

roasted beet salad

3 beets, with leaves
6 French shallots, unpeeled
6 garlic cloves, unpeeled
2 teaspoons vegetable oil
1 handful baby beet leaves
1/4 cup toasted walnuts

dressing

1 tablespoon red wine vinegar
2 tablespoons walnut oil
1 small garlic clove, crushed
1/2 teaspoon Dijon mustard

Preheat the oven to 400°F. Cut the leaves off the beets, wash well, and reserve. Scrub the bulbs, place in a roasting pan with the shallots and garlic cloves, and roast for 1 hour. Remove the shallots and garlic and roast the beets for another 30 minutes or until tender.

Whisk the dressing ingredients in a small bowl, then season well with sea salt and pepper. Slip the shallots and garlic from their skins into a large bowl. Peel the beets, cut them into wedges, and add them to the shallots. Gently mix the dressing through, then cool to room temperature.

Divide the beet mixture between two resealable containers and season well with sea salt and pepper. Pack the beet leaves and walnuts separately and mix them through the salad just before eating.

Makes 2 salads

Orange zest and basil add a lively counterpoint to the deep, mellow flavors of roasted vegetables and nutty brown rice.

brown rice, tuna, and roasted vegetable salad

1 small red bell pepper,
   roughly chopped
1 zucchini, thickly sliced
1 small onion, cut into wedges
2 tablespoons olive oil
2/3 cup brown rice (see Note)
6-oz. can tuna, drained

orange and basil dressing
zest of 1 orange
2 tablespoons orange juice
2 tablespoons olive oil
3 tablespoons torn basil leaves

Preheat the oven to 400°F. Put the bell pepper, zucchini, and onion in a baking dish. Pour over the oil, season with salt and black pepper, then toss to coat the vegetables with oil. Bake for 20 minutes or until lightly golden and soft, stirring once or twice during cooking.

Meanwhile, cook the rice according to the package instructions. Drain well, then rinse under cold water and drain again. Allow to cool in a sieve over a saucepan, fluffing up the grains with a fork occasionally.

While the rice is cooling, put all the orange and basil dressing ingredients in a small bowl and whisk well. Season with salt and black pepper.

Put the cooled rice in a bowl, then stir in the tuna and all the roasted vegetables. Pour over the dressing, gently toss together, and divide the salad between two resealable containers.

Note: You could also use leftover rice for this recipe. You will need about 1 1/2 cups of cold cooked brown rice.

Makes 2 salads

brown rice, tuna, and roasted vegetable salad

spicy tempeh salad

4 oz. spicy tempeh, cut
    into fine strips
2 teaspoons sesame oil
1/2 carrot
1/2 large red bell pepper
8 snow peas, trimmed
3–4 scallions
1 cup shredded red cabbage

1 tablespoon toasted
    sesame seeds
2 oz. crispy fried Chinese
    noodles

lime and chili dressing

1 garlic clove, crushed
2 teaspoons sweet chili sauce
1 tablespoon lime juice
1 1/2 tablespoons vegetable oil

Preheat the oven to 400°F. Put the tempeh on a nonstick baking sheet, brush lightly with the oil, and bake for 20 minutes.

Cut the carrot, bell pepper, snow peas, and scallions into julienne strips and toss in a bowl with the tempeh, cabbage, and sesame seeds. Whisk the dressing ingredients together in a small bowl, then drizzle over the salad. Toss to combine, then divide between two resealable containers. Pack the noodles separately and mix into the salad just before eating.

Makes 2 salads

salami pasta salad

1 baby fennel bulb, trimmed
1/2 small red bell pepper,
   thinly sliced
1/2 green bell pepper,
   thinly sliced
1 celery stalk, sliced
1/2 small red onion, thinly sliced
2 oz. thickly sliced pepper-
   coated salami
1 tablespoon chopped Italian
   parsley

4 oz. mixed colored fettuccine,
   broken into short pieces

dressing
1 1/2 tablespoons olive oil
1 tablespoon lemon juice
2 teaspoons Dijon mustard
1/4 teaspoon sugar
1 small garlic clove, crushed

Cut the fennel bulb in half, then slice thinly. Toss in a bowl with the bell peppers, celery, and onion. Cut the salami into strips and add to the salad along with the parsley.

Cook the pasta in a large pot of boiling salted water until al dente. Drain, rinse under cold water, then drain again. Add to the salad and gently toss everything together. Whisk the dressing ingredients in a small bowl and season with salt and plenty of cracked pepper. Pour over the salad, toss well to coat, then divide between two resealable containers.

Makes 2 salads

A handful of nuts, some gourmet mushrooms, and fresh, fiery ginger turn plain noodles into a sumptuous lunchtime surprise.

buckwheat noodle salad with shiitake and snow peas

4 oz. buckwheat noodles
2 tablespoons walnut pieces
1 tablespoon vegetable or olive oil
3/4 cup fresh shiitake mushrooms, stalks discarded,
    caps thinly sliced
1/2 cup snow peas, trimmed and finely sliced
3 scallions, finely sliced

sesame ginger dressing
1 tablespoon white wine vinegar
1/2 teaspoon sesame oil
2 tablespoons vegetable oil
3/4-inch piece of ginger, peeled and finely grated
1 small red chili, seeded and finely chopped

Cook the noodles according to the package instructions. Drain well, then rinse under cold running water, rubbing the noodles together gently to remove some of the starch. Drain well, then place in a bowl.

Meanwhile, put a frying pan over high heat. Add the walnuts and dry-fry for 2–3 minutes, shaking the pan now and then so the nuts color evenly. Remove, allow to cool, and roughly chop.

Heat the oil in the same pan, add the mushrooms, and sauté for about 2–3 minutes or until tender. Add them to the noodles with the snow peas, scallions, and chopped walnuts and gently mix together.

To make the sesame ginger dressing, put the vinegar, sesame oil, and vegetable oil in a small bowl and whisk until well combined. Stir in the ginger and chili, then drizzle over the noodles. Toss to combine, then divide the noodles between two resealable containers. Eat at room temperature.

Makes 2 salads

buckwheat noodle salad with shiitake and snow peas

tuna, bell pepper, and pasta salad

2 cups conchiglie or other
    shell-shaped pasta
1/2 cup green beans, trimmed
    and chopped
1 small red bell pepper,
    thinly sliced
1 scallion, sliced
1 large cucumber, thinly sliced
6 hard-boiled eggs, peeled
    and quartered
4 tomatoes, cut into eighths

6-oz. can tuna, drained
1/2 cup black olives
2 tablespoons chopped basil

dressing

1 tablespoon olive oil
3 tablespoons white wine
    vinegar
1 tablespoon lemon juice
1 garlic clove, crushed
1 teaspoon sugar

Cook the pasta in a large pot of boiling salted water until al dente, adding the beans for the final minute of cooking. Drain, rinse under cold water, and drain again. Place in a large bowl with the bell pepper and scallion and mix well. Add the cucumber, eggs, tomatoes, and tuna.

Combine all the dressing ingredients in a small screw-top jar and shake well. Drizzle half the dressing over the salad, then sprinkle the olives and basil over the top. Divide the salad between two resealable containers and drizzle with the remaining dressing.

Makes 2 salads

pastrami, mushroom, and cucumber salad

4 oz. lasagnette (mini lasagna
    sheets), broken into quarters
4 oz. sliced pastrami, cut
    into strips
1/2 celery stalk, sliced
1 tomato, cut into wedges
1/2 cucumber, thinly sliced
3/4 cup button mushrooms,
    thinly sliced
1/2 tablespoon finely
    chopped cilantro

dressing
1 1/2 tablespoons olive oil
1 tablespoon red wine vinegar
1/2 teaspoon Dijon mustard
1 garlic clove, crushed
a few drops of chili oil

Cook the pasta in a large pot of boiling salted water until al dente. Drain, rinse under cold water, and drain again. Allow to cool, then place in a large bowl with the pastrami, celery, tomato, cucumber, and mushrooms.

Combine all the dressing ingredients in a small screw-top jar and shake well. Toss the dressing through the salad, then cover and refrigerate for several hours to allow all the flavors to mingle. Adjust the seasoning, then divide between two resealable containers and sprinkle with the cilantro.

Makes 2 salads

For hungry days, this hearty salad is substantial but not too heavy, enlivened with green beans, fresh tomatoes, and olives.

Mediterranean potato salad

2 eggs

1 cup green beans, trimmed
 and cut into 1-inch lengths

3 waxy potatoes

1¹/2 cups penne, fusilli, or other
 pasta

2 firm, ripe tomatoes, seeded
 and diced

¹/4 cup Kalamata olives

anchovy dressing

3 tablespoons olive oil

1 tablespoon white wine
 vinegar

1 garlic clove, crushed

2 anchovy fillets, finely chopped

Bring a small saucepan of water to a boil. Add the eggs and cook for 7 minutes. Add the green beans and cook for an additional 2 minutes. Drain the eggs and beans and rinse under cold water. Allow to cool completely.

Meanwhile, put the potatoes in a pot of salted water and bring to a boil.

Cook for about 12 minutes or until the potatoes are tender when pierced with the tip of a sharp knife. Allow to cool slightly, then cut the potatoes into chunks and place in a large bowl.

Bring a separate pot of salted water to a boil and cook the pasta until al dente. Drain well, then add to the potatoes.

To make the anchovy dressing, whisk the oil and vinegar in a small bowl until well combined. Stir in the garlic and season with a little black pepper. Mash the anchovy into the dressing, mixing well. Pour the dressing over the potatoes and pasta while they are still warm and toss gently.

Peel the eggs and chop them into quarters. Add to the pasta with the beans, tomatoes, and olives. Mix gently and allow to cool completely, then divide the salad between two resealable containers.

Makes 2 salads

Mediterranean potato salad

lemon and vegetable pasta salad

1¹/2 cups farfalle
1 tablespoon olive oil
2 cups broccoli florets
¹/2 cup snow peas, trimmed
1 small yellow button squash,
    quartered
¹/2 celery stalk, finely sliced
2 teaspoons chopped chervil
8 chervil sprigs

dressing
1 tablespoon sour cream
2 teaspoons lemon juice
1 tablespoon olive oil
1 teaspoon finely grated
    lemon zest

Cook the pasta in a large pot of boiling salted water until al dente. Drain well, toss with 1 tablespoon of the oil, and set aside to cool.

Put the broccoli, snow peas, and squash in a large bowl, cover with boiling water, and let stand for 2 minutes. Drain, plunge into iced water, then drain again. Pat dry with paper towels and gently toss in a large bowl with the pasta and celery. Sprinkle the chopped chervil over the top.

Put all the dressing ingredients in a screw-top jar and shake well. Season to taste, then drizzle over the pasta and toss well. Divide between two resealable containers and sprinkle with chervil. Eat at room temperature.

Makes 2 salads

chef's salad

1 oz. Swiss cheese, cut into
 thin strips
2 thin slices of leg ham
3 oz. cooked chopped
 chicken or turkey
1 plum tomato, quartered

1 tablespoon chopped pimiento
1 hard-boiled egg, peeled
 and quartered
2 well-shaped lettuce leaves
3 tablespoons French dressing

Put the cheese, ham, chicken, tomato, pimiento, and egg in a bowl and gently toss to combine.

Wash and dry the lettuce leaves thoroughly. Arrange the salad inside the lettuce leaves and carefully place in two resealable containers. Pack the dressing separately and drizzle over the salad just before eating.

Makes 2 salads

Zinging with lime, fresh herbs, and chili, this wonderful salad is a true pick-me-up after a dull morning.

chicken noodle salad

4 oz. bean vermicelli noodles
1 tablespoon vegetable oil
1 garlic clove, crushed
1$\frac{1}{2}$-inch piece of fresh ginger, peeled and finely grated
1 green chili, seeded and finely chopped
9 oz. ground chicken
2 tablespoons lemon juice
2 kaffir lime leaves, shredded
1 tablespoon fish sauce
1 tablespoon chili sauce
2 tablespoons chopped cilantro leaves

Put the noodles in a large heatproof bowl, cover with boiling water, and soak for 5 minutes or until softened. Alternatively, cook the noodles according to the package instructions. Drain the noodles well, then rinse under cold water and drain again.

Heat the oil in a wok or frying pan over medium heat. Add the garlic, ginger, and chili and stir-fry for about 1 minute, being careful not to burn the garlic. Add the chicken and stir-fry for another 2–3 minutes. Stir in the lemon juice, lime leaves, fish sauce, and chili sauce and stir-fry for an additional minute. Remove from the heat and transfer to a large bowl.

Cut the noodles into shorter lengths with scissors. Add to the chicken mixture along with the cilantro and mix well. Allow to cool completely, then divide between two resealable containers.

Makes 2 salads

chicken noodle salad

Caesar salad

dressing
1 egg
1 garlic clove, crushed
1 anchovy fillet
1/4 teaspoon Worcestershire
    sauce
1 tablespoon lime juice
1/2 teaspoon Dijon mustard
3/4 cup olive oil

1/2 tablespoon butter
2 teaspoons olive oil
1 slice thick white bread, crust
    removed, cut into cubes
1 slice of Canadian bacon or
    rindless bacon
2 heads baby romaine lettuce,
    leaves washed and torn
1/3 cup shaved Parmesan cheese

To make the dressing, blend the egg, garlic, anchovy, Worcestershire sauce, lime juice, and mustard in a food processor until smooth. With the motor running, add the oil in a thin, steady stream until creamy. Season well.

Heat the butter and oil in a frying pan. Fry the bread over medium heat until crisp, about 5–8 minutes, then remove. Cook the bacon in the same pan for 3 minutes or until crispy, then break into bite-size pieces.

Divide the lettuce between two resealable containers and sprinkle with the Parmesan. Pack the dressing in a separate container, and the bacon and croutons in another container. Add them to the salad just before eating.

Makes 2 salads

chicken, pear, and pasta salad

1 1/2 cups gemelli, fusilli, or
    other spiral pasta
4 oz. boneless, skinless chicken
    breasts
1 pear, cored and thinly sliced
2 scallions, finely sliced, plus
    extra, to serve

1 tablespoon toasted
    slivered almonds
2 oz. creamy blue cheese
1 1/2 tablespoons sour cream

Cook the pasta in a large pot of boiling salted water until al dente. Drain, rinse under cold water, and drain again. Allow to cool.

Put the chicken in a frying pan, cover with cold water, and simmer gently for 8 minutes or until tender, turning occasionally. Remove from the pan, allow to cool, then slice finely and place in a bowl with the cooled pasta. Add the pear, scallions, and almonds.

Put the blue cheese and sour cream in a food processor with a large pinch each of salt and pepper and 1 1/2 tablespoons of ice water. Blend until smooth. Pour the mixture over the salad and gently toss to coat. Divide between two resealable containers and sprinkle with scallions.

Makes 2 salads

Caramelized leek and lightly melted crumbs of creamy blue cheese lend a savory sophistication to this simple pasta dish.

pasta salad with caramelized vegetables

2 tablespoons olive oil
2 celery stalks, sliced
1 small onion, halved and
 thinly sliced
1 garlic clove, crushed
pinch of sugar
2 leeks, white part only, sliced
2 cups pasta shells or bows
2 tablespoons toasted pine nuts

3 oz. soft blue cheese, such as
 Gorgonzola, crumbled

dressing
1 tablespoon olive oil
1 tablespoon chopped
 Italian parsley
1 tablespoon lemon juice

Heat the oil in a frying pan. Add the celery and onion, then cover and cook over medium heat for 5 minutes, stirring occasionally. Stir in the garlic, sugar, and leeks. Reduce the heat, cover the pan, and gently cook, stirring occasionally, for another 10 minutes or until the vegetables are golden brown and soft. Remove the lid, increase the heat, and cook the

vegetables for another 2–3 minutes or until light golden, being careful not to burn them. Season with salt and black pepper, then set aside.

Meanwhile, cook the pasta in a large pot of boiling salted water until al dente. Drain well, then, while the pasta is still warm, add the caramelized vegetables and set aside.

Put the dressing ingredients in a small bowl, season with salt and black pepper, and mix well. Pour over the pasta, stir in the pine nuts and cheese, and toss gently. Allow to cool, then divide between two resealable containers. This salad is equally delicious cold or warmed up in a microwave.

Makes 2 salads

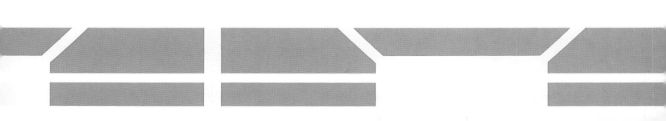

pasta salad with caramelized vegetables

asparagus and orange salad

1 bunch thin asparagus spears	**orange poppy seed dressing**
1 cup watercress leaves	$1/2$ tablespoon orange juice
$1/4$ small red onion, very thinly sliced	$1/2$ teaspoon finely grated orange zest
1 small orange, peeled and cut into 12 segments	$1/2$ teaspoon sugar
2 oz. soft goat cheese	$1/2$ tablespoon red wine vinegar
	1 teaspoon poppy seeds
	1 tablespoon olive oil

Bring a pot of lightly salted water to a boil, add the asparagus, and blanch for 1–2 minutes or until bright green and just tender. Drain and refresh under cold water, then drain again.

Gently toss the asparagus in a bowl with the watercress, onion, and orange segments. Divide the salad between two resealable containers and crumble the goat cheese on top. Season to taste with salt and pepper.

To make the orange poppy seed dressing, mix together the orange juice, orange zest, sugar, vinegar, and poppy seeds, then whisk in the oil. Pack the dressing separately and drizzle over the salad just before eating.

Makes 2 salads

cucumber, feta, mint, and dill salad

2 cucumbers
4 oz. feta cheese, cubed
1/2 small red onion, thinly sliced
1 tablespoon finely chopped dill
1/2 tablespoon dried mint
1 1/2 tablespoons olive oil
1 tablespoon lemon juice

Peel the cucumbers, scoop out the seeds, then cut the flesh into 1/2-inch cubes. Gently toss in a bowl with the feta, onion, and dill.

Grind the mint to a powder with a mortar and pestle, or force it through a sieve. Place in a small bowl with the oil and lemon juice, then season with salt and black pepper and mix well. Drizzle the dressing over the salad, toss well, then divide between two resealable containers.

Makes 2 salads

This inventive dish with chicken, corn, and rice shows you need never compromise on quality if you're in a hurry.

rice salad with chicken

3/4 cup jasmine rice
4 oz. roasted or grilled chicken
1/2 cucumber, seeded and diced
2 cups grape tomatoes, halved
4 scallions, sliced
11-oz. can corn kernels, drained

dressing
3 tablespoons olive oil
1 tablespoon lemon juice
1 tablespoon honey
1 teaspoon Dijon mustard
1 small red chili, seeded and sliced

Cook the rice in a large pot of boiling water until just tender. Drain well, briefly rinse under cold water, then drain again. Leave in a sieve over a saucepan, fluffing up the grains occasionally with a fork. While the rice is still warm, place it in a bowl while you make the dressing.

Whisk all the dressing ingredients together thoroughly in a small bowl, season with salt and black pepper, and pour over the warm rice. Mix well, then cover and refrigerate until cooled completely.

Shred the chicken into bite-size pieces and mix into the rice with the cucumber, tomatoes, scallions, and corn kernels. Season to taste, then divide between two resealable containers.

Makes 2 salads

rice salad with chicken

warm winter Long cold evenings and chilly weekends stoke up the appetite for good square meals that will warm you up without weighing you down. So when the mercury starts dropping, fire up your enthusiasm and head straight for the kitchen. Whip on your apron, crank up your creativity, rustle up a wonderful warm salad, and before long you'll feel a glow of contentment from top to toe.

The concept of cold and raw may be refreshing and appealing when the temperature is soaring and eating can seem a chore. But as night comes ever earlier and you find yourself ferreting for last year's sweaters and thick woolly socks, it takes a little something extra to make a satisfying meal. Roasts, stews, and casseroles naturally have their place in any winter repertoire, but satisfying doesn't have to mean stodgy. Weekend lunches, dinner for one, and late-night meals after a long day at work are the prime times when many of us sneak off to pick up some takeout or settle for the short-lived comfort of a grilled cheese sandwich in front of the television. But when preparing a full-blown meal seems off-putting and it's tempting to take to the couch and reach for the phone to order a lard-laden home delivery, don't despair: this is when the warm salad comes into its own. Healthy rather than worthy, the best warm salads take the finest produce of the season and turn winter's harvest into delectable, satisfying meals that nourish the soul as well as the body. Comfort food comes in all shapes and sizes and warm salads deserve to figure highly on the list. This is seriously good food that needn't involve an assembly line of ingredients and cooks. Warm, salty prosciutto, oozy melted cheese, and fresh, delicate greens are all the more enticing when quickly cooked. Roasting root vegetables, onions, and garlic brings a mellow warmth and caramelized sweetness that is infinitely soothing on a cold, dark evening—and as an added bonus, the hot oven turns a cold house into a cozy cocoon filled with heartening aromas. So it's time to welcome in food that is deeply invigorating—a celebration of winter and the opportunity for reflection and the quiet contemplation that it brings.

scallop salad with saffron dressing

saffron dressing
pinch of saffron threads
1/4 cup mayonnaise
1 1/2 tablespoons cream
1 teaspoon lemon juice

20 scallops, with roe
2 tablespoons butter
1 tablespoon olive oil
2 cups mixed salad leaves
1 small handful chervil leaves

To make the saffron dressing, put the saffron in a bowl and soak in 2 teaspoons of hot water for 10 minutes. Add the mayonnaise, mixing well, until the mixture becomes rich yellow in color. Stir in the cream, then the lemon juice. Refrigerate until needed.

Slice or pull off any veins, membranes, or hard white muscles from the scallops, leaving the roe attached. Rinse the scallops and pat them dry with paper towels. Heat the butter and oil in a large frying pan over high heat and sear the scallops in small batches for 1 minute on each side.

Divide the salad leaves and chervil between four serving plates, then top each with five scallops. Drizzle the dressing on top and serve.

Serves 4

scallop and potato with preserved lemon dressing

preserved lemon dressing
1/2 preserved lemon
3 tablespoons olive oil
2 tablespoons lemon juice
1 tablespoon sweet chili sauce
2 tablespoons white wine
   vinegar
2 tablespoons chopped cilantro

vegetable oil, for pan-frying
3 potatoes, peeled and sliced
   paper thin
1 1/2 lb. scallops, without roe
2 tablespoons olive oil
1 1/2 cups baby spinach leaves

First, make the dressing. Scoop out and discard the pulp from the preserved lemon, wash the rind well, and thinly slice it. Place in a bowl with the remaining dressing ingredients and whisk together well.

Heat 3/4 inch of oil in a deep, heavy-based frying pan and cook the potato in batches over medium heat for 1–2 minutes or until crisp and golden. Drain on crumpled paper towels.

Rinse the scallops and pat them dry. Heat some oil in a frying pan and cook the scallops in batches over high heat for 1 minute on each side, until golden. Serve on a bed of spinach and potato, drizzled with the dressing.

Serves 4

Tender quarters of artichoke hearts enveloped in crispy, golden bread crumbs make this dish an adorable winter treat.

prosciutto and arugula with Parmesan-crusted artichokes

4 globe artichokes
1 lemon, halved
2 eggs, lightly beaten
1/4 cup fresh bread crumbs
1/4 cup grated Parmesan cheese
vegetable oil, for pan-frying
1 tablespoon olive oil
8 slices of prosciutto

1 tablespoon white wine
   vinegar
1 garlic clove, crushed
1 bunch arugula, trimmed
shaved Parmesan cheese,
   to serve

Remove the tough outer leaves from the artichokes, down to the pale leaves. Slice off the tops, halfway down the tough leaves. Trim the stems to 1 1/2 inches long, then peel lightly. Halve each artichoke lengthwise and remove the hairy choke with a spoon. Rub the artichokes with the lemon while you work and place in a bowl of cold water mixed with lemon juice to keep them from turning brown. Cut them into quarters, place in a large pot of boiling water, and cook for 2 minutes, then drain.

Whisk the eggs in a bowl, and combine the seasoned bread crumbs and grated Parmesan in another bowl. Dip each artichoke quarter into the egg, then roll in the bread crumb mixture to coat.

Heat 3/4 inch of oil in a deep, heavy-based frying pan. Add the artichokes in batches and fry over medium heat for 2–3 minutes or until golden. Remove and drain on crumpled paper towels.

Heat the olive oil in a nonstick frying pan. Cook the prosciutto in two batches over medium heat for 2 minutes or until crisp. Remove the prosciutto with tongs, leaving the oil in the pan. Mix the vinegar and garlic into the pan oil with a little salt and pepper to use as a dressing.

Put the arugula in a bowl, add half the dressing, and toss well. Divide the arugula, artichokes, and prosciutto between four plates and drizzle with the remaining dressing. Sprinkle with Parmesan and sea salt, and serve.

Serves 4

scallop salad with saffron dressing

scallop salad with lime and ginger

dressing
3 tablespoons peanut oil
1 tablespoon lime juice
1 tablespoon grated fresh
    ginger
1/2 teaspoon honey
1 tablespoon chopped cilantro

3 zucchini, julienned
2 carrots, julienned
2 scallions, sliced diagonally
14 oz. scallops, without roe
1 tablespoon peanut oil

Put all the dressing ingredients in a small screw-top jar and shake well. Arrange the zucchini, carrots, and scallions on four serving plates.

Slice or pull off any veins, membranes, or hard white muscles from the scallops. Rinse the scallops and pat them dry with paper towels.

Heat the oil in a heavy-based pan. Add the scallops and cook in small batches over high heat for 1 minute on each side or until golden. Remove from the pan and keep warm while cooking the remaining batches.

Pile the scallops over the vegetables, drizzle with the dressing, and serve.

Serves 4

Thai-style chicken salad

4 boneless, skinless
   chicken breasts, cut
   into 1/2-inch strips
1 teaspoon grated fresh ginger
1 garlic clove, crushed
2 tablespoons soy sauce
1 tablespoon peanut oil
3 scallions, sliced diagonally

2 carrots, julienned
1/3 cup snow pea sprouts

dressing
2 tablespoons sweet chili sauce
1 tablespoon rice vinegar
2 tablespoons peanut oil

Put the chicken in a nonmetallic dish. Mix together the ginger, garlic, and soy sauce and smother the mixture all over the chicken. Cover and refrigerate for at least 2 hours—preferably overnight—turning occasionally.

Nearer to serving time, put all the dressing ingredients in a small screw-top jar and shake well.

Heat the oil in a heavy-based pan. Add the chicken and cook in batches over medium heat for 3–4 minutes or until cooked and well browned. Drain on crumpled paper towels and set aside to cool, then place in a serving bowl with the scallions, carrots, and snow pea sprouts. Pour the dressing on top and toss lightly to combine. Serve immediately.

Serves 4

Soft and gooey, warm and salty, pan-fried haloumi is heavenly piled high on crusty, buttery garlic bread.

haloumi salad and warm garlic bread

4 firm ripe tomatoes
1 cucumber
1 bunch arugula, trimmed
1/2 cup Kalamata olives
1 whole loaf crusty white bread
2 tablespoons olive oil
1 large garlic clove, cut in half
14 oz. haloumi cheese, cut into
    8 slices

dressing
1 tablespoon lemon juice
1 tablespoon chopped fresh
    oregano
3 tablespoons olive oil

Cut the tomatoes and cucumber into bite-size chunks and toss in a serving dish with the arugula and olives. Mix well.

Whisk together the dressing ingredients in a small bowl, season to taste with salt and freshly cracked pepper, and set aside.

Slice the bread into eight $1/2$-inch slices. Drizzle the bread with $1^1/2$ tablespoons of the oil and season with salt and pepper. Cook under a hot broiler for about 1–2 minutes on each side or until lightly golden, then thoroughly rub each slice with a cut side of the garlic. Wrap the bread loosely in foil and keep in a warm oven.

Heat the remaining oil in a frying pan and fry the haloumi over medium heat for 1–2 minutes on each side or until golden brown.

Pour half the dressing over the salad and toss well. Arrange the haloumi on top and drizzle with the rest of the dressing. Serve immediately with the warm garlic bread.

Serves 4

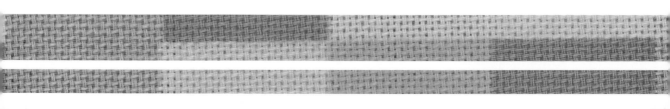

Thai-style chicken salad

roasted mushroom and goat cheese salad

6 large-cap mushrooms,
   stems removed
1 tablespoon chopped thyme
3 garlic cloves, finely chopped
1½ tablespoons olive oil
1 cup baby arugula leaves
4 oz. goat cheese

1½ tablespoons chopped
   Italian parsley

lemon dressing
1½ tablespoons lemon juice
2 tablespoons olive oil
½ teaspoon grated lemon zest

Preheat the oven to 400°F. Put the mushrooms on a large baking sheet, sprinkle with the thyme and garlic, then drizzle with the oil. Cover with foil and roast for 20 minutes. Take the mushrooms out of the oven, give them a good toss to mix the flavors through, then put the foil back on and roast for another 10 minutes or until cooked.

Meanwhile, put the dressing ingredients in a small bowl and whisk well.

Spread the arugula on a serving platter. Cut the mushrooms in half and arrange them over the arugula. Crumble the goat cheese on top. Give the dressing another quick whisk and drizzle it over the salad. Sprinkle with parsley and serve while warm.

Serves 4

goat cheese toasts with arugula salad

12 slices white bread
4 rounds of goat cheese
1 cup mixed salad leaves
1/2 small bunch arugula,
   trimmed
2 cups cherry tomatoes, halved
1 tablespoon snipped chives

dressing
1 tablespoon white wine
   vinegar
3 tablespoons olive oil
1/2 teaspoon whole-grain
   mustard

Preheat the oven to 350°F. Find a cookie cutter the same size as the goat cheese and cut a round out of each slice of bread. (The bread needs to be the same diameter as the cheese so the edges won't burn under the broiler.) Put the bread on a baking sheet and bake for 10 minutes.

Slice each piece of goat cheese into three rounds, then place a slice on each piece of toasted bread. Cook under a hot broiler for 5 minutes or until the cheese turns golden and bubbles.

Arrange the salad greens and cherry tomatoes on four small serving plates. Whisk the dressing ingredients in a small bowl and drizzle over the salad. Arrange three cheese rounds on each plate, sprinkle with chives, and serve.

Serves 4

Toasted hazelnut and sweet, juicy orange make this simple salad an appetizing base for meltingly warm goat cheese.

warm goat cheese salad with orange and hazelnut

hazelnut dressing
1/4 cup hazelnuts
1 tablespoon orange juice
1 tablespoon lemon juice
1/2 cup olive oil

2 oranges
1/2 bunch watercress
1 cup baby spinach leaves
olive oil, for brushing
11 oz. goat cheese, sliced into
    4 portions

Preheat the oven to 350°F. To make the dressing, put the hazelnuts on a baking sheet and roast for 5–6 minutes or until the skins turn dark brown. Wrap the hazelnuts in a clean dish towel and rub them together to remove the skins, then put them in a food processor with the orange juice, lemon juice, and a pinch of salt. With the motor running, gradually add the oil a few drops at a time. When about half the oil has been incorporated, add the remainder in a steady stream.

Peel the rind and bitter white pith from the oranges. Cut the flesh into segments between the membrane, removing the seeds. Put the segments in a large bowl with the watercress, spinach, and 2 tablespoons of the dressing. Toss well and season to taste with pepper.

Heat a small, nonstick frying pan and brush lightly with olive oil. Carefully press each slice of goat cheese firmly into the pan and cook over medium heat for 1–2 minutes or until a crust forms underneath.

Arrange half the salad over four serving plates and put the goat cheese slices on top, crust side up. Sprinkle with the remaining salad, drizzle with the remaining dressing, and serve at once.

Serves 4

warm goat cheese salad with orange and hazelnut

spinach salad with bacon and quail eggs

12 quail eggs
2 1/2 tablespoons vegetable oil
4 slices of Canadian bacon,
    cut into thin strips
2 tablespoons apple cider
    vinegar
2 garlic cloves, crushed
1 teaspoon Dijon mustard

1 teaspoon maple syrup
1/2 teaspoon Worcestershire
    sauce
2 cups baby spinach leaves
7-oz. carton cherry tomatoes,
    halved
1/3 cup toasted pine nuts

Bring a small saucepan of water to a boil. Carefully add the quail eggs and simmer for 1 1/2 minutes. Drain, then rinse under cold running water until cool. Carefully peel the eggs and cut them in half.

Heat a little of the oil in a nonstick frying pan. Add the bacon and gently cook for 5 minutes or until crisp. Remove with tongs, leaving the oil behind, and drain the bacon on crumpled paper towels. Add the vinegar, garlic, mustard, maple syrup, and Worcestershire to the pan and gently swirl for 2 minutes or until bubbling. Add the remaining oil and heat for 1 minute.

Layer the spinach, bacon, tomatoes, and pine nuts in a salad bowl. Add the quail eggs, pour the warm dressing over, season to taste, and serve.

Serves 4

ricotta toasts with pear and walnut salad

1 small French baguette,
    cut into 16 thin slices
vegetable oil, for brushing
1 garlic clove, cut in half
1 cup walnuts
2 pears, cored and diced
2 tablespoons lime juice

4 cups mixed salad leaves
1 cup ricotta cheese

lime vinaigrette
3 tablespoons lime juice
3 tablespoons oil
2 tablespoons raspberry vinegar

Preheat the oven to 350°F. Brush the bread with a little oil, rub with the cut side of the garlic, spread on a baking sheet, and bake for 10 minutes or until golden. Bake the walnuts for 5 minutes or until lightly browned, turning to ensure even coloring. Cool for 5 minutes.

Whisk the vinaigrette ingredients in a small bowl with 1 teaspoon salt and $1/2$ teaspoon freshly ground black pepper. Put the pear cubes in a bowl, add the lime juice, and mix well. Add the vinaigrette, salad leaves, and walnuts, toss well, then divide among four serving bowls.

Spread the toasts with ricotta and cook under a hot broiler for 2–3 minutes or until hot. Arrange four slices on each plate and serve.

Serves 4

These tantalizingly tender slices of perfectly pink, peppery lamb are almost worth sacrificing summer for.

Greek peppered lamb salad

$1\frac{1}{2}$ tablespoons black pepper
11 oz. lamb tenderloin
1 tablespoon olive oil
3 vine-ripened tomatoes,
    each cut into 8 wedges
2 cucumbers, sliced
$3/4$ cup marinated Kalamata
    olives, drained (reserve
    $1\frac{1}{2}$ tablespoons of the oil
    for the dressing)
4 oz. feta cheese, cubed
$1/2$ teaspoon dried oregano

dressing
$1/4$ teaspoon dried oregano
1 tablespoon lemon juice
1 tablespoon extra-virgin
    olive oil

Sprinkle the pepper in a small, shallow dish large enough to hold the lamb. Roll the lamb around in the pepper, pressing the pepper on with your fingers. Cover and refrigerate for 15 minutes.

Heat the oil in a frying pan or charbroil pan. Cook the lamb over high heat for 2–3 minutes on each side or until cooked to your liking. Remove from the heat, cover with foil, and keep in a warm place.

Gently toss the tomatoes, cucumbers, olives, feta, and oregano together in a bowl. Put the dressing ingredients in a small bowl, add the reserved oil from the olives, and whisk well. Season to taste, then pour half the dressing over the salad. Toss well, then arrange on a serving platter.

Cut the lamb diagonally into $1/2$-inch-thick slices and arrange on top of the salad. Pour the remaining dressing over the top and serve.

Serves 4

spinach salad with bacon and quail eggs

fava bean, mint, and bacon salad

1¹/₄ lb. frozen fava beans,
   defrosted
9 oz. piece of Kasseler
   or pancetta (see Note)
1 tablespoon olive oil
¹/₂ butter lettuce, shredded
2 large handfuls mint, shredded
4 flatbreads

dressing
1¹/₂ teaspoons Dijon mustard
1 teaspoon sugar
2 tablespoons white wine
   vinegar
3 tablespoons extra-virgin
   olive oil

Cook the beans in a pot of lightly salted boiling water for 2–3 minutes or until tender. Drain, refresh under cold water, and remove the skins.

Slice the Kasseler or pancetta into 3/4-inch chunks. Heat the oil in a heavy-based frying pan and fry on all sides for 3–4 minutes or until golden. Toss in a large bowl with the beans, lettuce, and mint.

To make the dressing, combine the mustard, sugar, and vinegar in a small bowl. Whisk in the oil and season to taste. Pile the salad onto fresh or lightly toasted flatbreads, drizzle with dressing, and serve.

Note: Kasseler is a German smoked pork loin sold in some delicatessens.

Serves 4

warm potato salad with green olive dressing

8 small, waxy potatoes (such
    as fingerling), scrubbed

green olive dressing
1/3 cup green olives, pitted and
    finely chopped
1 teaspoon capers, rinsed,
    drained, and finely chopped

1 large handful parsley,
    finely chopped
1 1/2 tablespoons lemon juice
1 teaspoon finely grated
    lemon zest
2 garlic cloves, crushed
4 tablespoons extra-virgin
    olive oil

Put the potatoes in a pot of cold, lightly salted water. Bring to a boil, then reduce the heat and simmer for 12–15 minutes or until tender when pierced with a sharp knife. Drain and allow to cool slightly.

While the potatoes are cooking, put all the green olive dressing ingredients in a small bowl and whisk together well with a fork.

While the potatoes are still warm, cut them in half, transfer to a large serving bowl, and gently toss the dressing through. Season to taste with fresh black pepper, and a little salt if needed.

Serves 4

347

Don't grumble when the weather hits an all-time low. This homely, humble salad will cheer the very cockles of your soul.

sausage and egg salad with anchovy dressing

4 eggs
2 cups green beans, trimmed
   and halved
2 tablespoons olive oil
4 good-quality sausages,
   cut into 1/2-inch slices
2 thick slices crusty white
   bread, crusts removed,
   cut into 1/2-inch cubes
4 cups mixed salad leaves

3/4 cup roasted red bell pepper,
   sliced

anchovy dressing
1 garlic clove, crushed
3 tablespoons olive oil
2 tablespoons lemon juice
3 anchovy fillets, finely chopped
2 tablespoons shredded basil
   leaves

Bring a small saucepan of water to a boil, add the eggs, and cook for 5 minutes. Add the beans and cook for an additional 2 minutes. Drain and rinse the eggs and beans under cold water, draining the beans well. Crack the egg shells slightly and cool in cold water.

Meanwhile, heat half the oil in a frying pan. Add the sausage slices and fry over medium heat for about 5 minutes or until golden and cooked, turning once. Remove from the pan using a slotted spoon and set aside.

Put the frying pan back over medium heat and add the remaining oil. When the oil is hot, add the bread cubes and fry, turning now and then, for about 2 minutes or until golden on all sides.

Put all the anchovy dressing ingredients in a small bowl. Mash the anchovies well, mix thoroughly, then season with black pepper and set aside.

Once the eggs have cooled, peel them and then cut them into quarters. Put the sausages, beans, salad leaves, and bell pepper in a serving bowl. Add the dressing and toss gently. Top with the eggs and croutons and serve.

Serves 4

sausage and egg salad with anchovy dressing

mixed salad with warm Brie dressing

1/2 sourdough baguette
3/4 cup olive oil
6 slices bacon
2 garlic cloves, peeled
2 heads baby romaine lettuce,
    leaves separated
2 cups baby spinach leaves
1/2 cup toasted pine nuts

2 French shallots, finely chopped
1 tablespoon Dijon mustard
4 tablespoons sherry vinegar
10 oz. ripe Brie cheese, rind
    removed

Preheat the oven to 350°F. Thinly slice the baguette and brush each slice all over with some of the oil. Spread on a baking sheet and bake for 20 minutes or until golden. Bake the bacon on a separate sheet for 4 minutes or until crisp, then break into pieces and allow to cool.

Rub the top of each toasted bread slice with one garlic clove, cut in half. Toss in a large bowl with the bacon, lettuce, spinach, and pine nuts.

Heat the remaining oil in a frying pan. Add the shallots and gently cook for 1–2 minutes to soften. Crush the remaining garlic clove and add to the pan with the mustard and vinegar. Gently whisk in the Brie until it has melted. Pour the warm dressing over the salad, toss gently, and serve.

Serves 4

roasted tomato, bacon, and pasta salad

3 cups cherry tomatoes
6 garlic cloves, unpeeled
2 tablespoons olive oil
4 1/2 cups pasta, such as penne
6 slices rindless smoked bacon
6 oz. feta cheese, crumbled

1/2 cup Kalamata olives
1 large handful shredded basil

Preheat the oven to 350°F. Put the tomatoes and garlic in a roasting dish and drizzle with the oil. Season, toss lightly to coat, then bake for 15–20 minutes (reserve the roasting juices). Meanwhile, cook the pasta in a large pot of boiling salted water until al dente. Drain well.

Put a nonstick frying pan over high heat. Add the bacon and cook for 4–5 minutes or until crispy. Remove the bacon with tongs, leaving all the pan juices behind, then chop into strips. Swish some of the pasta around the frying pan to soak up all the pan juices. Season with salt and pepper if needed, then empty into a large serving bowl with the rest of the pasta, the bacon, roasted tomatoes, feta, and olives. Toss gently.

Squeeze the garlic cloves from their skins and mix them with the roasted tomato juices. Toss through the pasta, sprinkle with basil, and serve warm.

Serves 4

beef satay salad

2 teaspoons tamarind pulp
$1/2$ teaspoon sesame oil
2 tablespoons soy sauce
2 teaspoons brown sugar
2 garlic cloves, crushed
1 tablespoon lime juice
$1^1/2$ lb. sirloin steak
1 tablespoon peanut oil
6 large romaine lettuce leaves,
   shredded
1 red bell pepper, julienned
2 cups bean sprouts, trimmed
2 tablespoons crisp fried onion

satay sauce
2 red chilies, chopped
$1/2$ teaspoon shrimp paste
1 garlic clove
6 red Asian shallots
2 teaspoons peanut oil
1 cup coconut milk
1 tablespoon lime juice
$3/4$ cup unsalted roasted
   peanuts, finely ground in
   a food processor
1 tablespoon kecap manis
1 tablespoon brown sugar
1 tablespoon fish sauce
2 kaffir lime leaves, shredded

Mix the tamarind pulp with 3 tablespoons of boiling water, then allow it to cool. Mash the pulp with your fingertips to dissolve it, then strain well, reserving the liquid. Discard the pulp.

Put the sesame oil, soy sauce, sugar, garlic, lime juice, and 2 tablespoons of the tamarind water in a large nonmetallic bowl. Add the beef, turn to coat, then cover with plastic wrap. Chill for 2 hours, turning occasionally.

Meanwhile, make the satay sauce. Put the chilies, shrimp paste, garlic, and shallots in a food processor and blend to a paste. Heat the peanut oil in a frying pan and cook the paste over medium heat for 3 minutes. Add the remaining tamarind water and remaining satay sauce ingredients and cook until thickened. Thin with $1/2$ cup water, then return to a boil for 2 minutes. Season to taste.

About 30 minutes before you're ready to eat, remove the beef from the fridge to bring it to room temperature. Heat the peanut oil in a frying pan. Cook the beef over high heat for about 3 minutes on each side or until medium-rare. Remove from the heat, cover with foil, and let stand in a warm place for 3 minutes, then thinly slice. Toss in a large bowl with the lettuce, bell pepper, and bean sprouts. Pile onto serving plates, drizzle with the satay sauce, then sprinkle with fried onion flakes and serve.

Serves 4

roasted tomato, bacon, and pasta salad

spinach and avocado salad with warm mustard

1/2 bunch spinach	2 teaspoons sesame seeds
1 red- or green-leaf lettuce	1 tablespoon lemon juice
2 small avocados, thinly sliced	2 teaspoons whole-grain
3 tablespoons olive oil	mustard

Strip the stalks from the spinach and discard the outer leaves of the lettuce. Wash and thoroughly dry the spinach and lettuce leaves and tear them into bite-size pieces. Put them in a large serving bowl and add the avocado slices.

Heat 1 tablespoon of the oil in a small pan. Add the sesame seeds and fry over low heat until they just start to turn golden—this won't take long. Remove from the heat immediately and allow to cool slightly.

Add the remaining oil, lemon juice, and mustard to the pan and stir well. Pour the warm dressing over the salad, toss gently to coat the leaves, and serve immediately.

Serves 4

warm lima bean salad

2 tablespoons olive oil
1 onion, finely chopped
1 garlic clove, crushed
1 small red bell pepper, cut
    into short strips
3/4 cup green beans, trimmed
8–10 button mushrooms, sliced

1 tablespoon balsamic vinegar
15-oz. can lima beans
chopped parsley, to serve

Heat half the oil in a frying pan. Add the onion and gently stir for about 2 minutes over medium heat. Add the garlic, bell pepper, green beans, mushrooms, and vinegar, then cook for 5 minutes, stirring occasionally.

Thoroughly rinse and drain the lima beans. Add them to the pan with the remaining oil and stir until just warmed through. Sprinkle with the chopped parsley and serve.

Serves 4

shrimp and cannellini bean salad

1 cup dried cannellini beans
2 red bell peppers
2 1/2 cups baby green beans
1/2 loaf day-old Italian or
   other crusty bread
4 tablespoons olive oil
1 large garlic clove, finely
   chopped
2 1/4 lb. raw shrimp, peeled and
   deveined, tails intact
1 large handful Italian parsley,
   roughly chopped

lemon and caper dressing
3 tablespoons lemon juice
3 tablespoons olive oil
2 tablespoons capers, rinsed,
   drained, and chopped
1 teaspoon sugar, optional

Soak the cannellini beans in plenty of cold water for at least 8 hours, or overnight if possible. Drain the beans, rinse them well, then put them in a pot and cover with plenty of fresh, cold water. Bring to a boil, then reduce the heat and simmer for 20–30 minutes, or until tender. Drain, rinse under cold water, then drain again and put in a serving bowl.

Cut the bell peppers into large flat pieces and remove the seeds and membranes. Cook, skin side up, under a hot broiler until the skins blacken and blister. Allow to cool in a plastic bag, then peel away the skin and cut the flesh into strips. Add them to the cannellini beans.

Bring a saucepan of lightly salted water to a boil, add the green beans, and blanch until bright green and just tender, about 2–3 minutes. Drain and add to the serving bowl.

Put all the lemon and caper dressing ingredients in a screw-top jar and shake well. Season to taste and set aside.

Cut the bread into six slices, then cut each slice into quarters. Heat 3 tablespoons of the oil in a frying pan and fry the bread slices over medium heat for a minute or two on each side until golden. Remove.

Heat the remaining oil in the frying pan, add the garlic and shrimp, and cook for 2–3 minutes or until the shrimp turn opaque. Mix the shrimp into the salad with the dressing, toasted bread, and parsley and serve.

Serves 4

shrimp and cannellini bean salad

warm casarecci and sweet potato salad

1¹/₂ lb. orange sweet potato, peeled and cut into chunks

2 tablespoons olive oil

1 lb. casarecci or bow tie pasta

11-oz. jar marinated feta cheese, in oil

3 tablespoons balsamic vinegar

1 bunch asparagus, trimmed and sliced

1 cup baby arugula or baby spinach leaves

2 ripe tomatoes, chopped

¹/₄ cup toasted pine nuts

Preheat the oven to 400°F. Put the sweet potato in a roasting pan, drizzle with the oil, season liberally, and bake for 20 minutes or until tender. Meanwhile, cook the pasta in a large pot of boiling salted water until al dente. Drain well and place in a serving bowl.

Drain 3 tablespoons of oil from the feta and whisk it together with the vinegar to make a dressing.

Boil, steam, or microwave the asparagus until bright green and just tender. Drain, refresh in cold water, and drain again. Add to the pasta with the sweet potato, arugula, feta, tomatoes, and pine nuts. Pour the dressing over and toss gently. Season with black pepper and serve.

Serves 4

warm artichoke salad

8 young globe artichokes
    (about 7 oz. each)
1 lemon, halved
2^1/$_2$ handfuls basil leaves,
    shredded
^{1}/$_2$ cup shaved Parmesan
    cheese

dressing
1 garlic clove, finely chopped
^{1}/$_2$ teaspoon sugar
1 teaspoon Dijon mustard
2 teaspoons finely chopped
    lemon zest
3 tablespoons lemon juice
4 tablespoons extra-virgin
    olive oil

Remove the tough outer leaves from the artichokes, down to the pale leaves. Slice off the tops, halfway down the tough leaves. Trim the stems to 1^1/$_2$ inches long and lightly peel them. Cut the artichokes in half lengthwise and remove the hairy choke with a spoon. Rub each one with lemon while you work and place in a bowl of cold water mixed with lemon juice to prevent them from turning brown. Put the artichokes in a large pot of boiling water, top with a plate or heatproof bowl to keep them immersed, then cook for 25 minutes or until tender. Drain and cut in half.

To make the dressing, mix the garlic, sugar, mustard, lemon zest, and lemon juice in a small bowl. Season with salt and freshly ground black pepper, then whisk in the oil with a fork until combined. Pour over the warm artichokes and sprinkle with the basil and Parmesan.

Serves 4

The distinctive peppery notes of horseradish, watercress, and black pepper strike a sterling chord with subtle, salty salmon.

pepper-crusted salmon salad

1 tablespoon coarsely ground black pepper
4 salmon fillets (about 6 oz. each), skin removed
1/3 cup mayonnaise
1 1/2 tablespoons lemon juice
2 teaspoons creamed horseradish
1 small garlic clove, crushed
2 tablespoons chopped parsley
3 heaping cups watercress
3 tablespoons olive oil
2 tablespoons butter
8 butter lettuce leaves, torn

Mix the pepper in a bowl with 1/4 teaspoon salt. Use the mixture to coat both sides of each salmon fillet, pressing the pepper down firmly with your fingers. Cover and refrigerate for 30 minutes.

Put the mayonnaise in a food processor with the lemon juice, horseradish, garlic, parsley, half the watercress, 1 tablespoon of the oil, and 1 tablespoon of warm water. Blend for 1 minute.

Heat the butter and 1 tablespoon of the oil in a large frying pan until bubbling. Add the salmon fillets and cook over medium heat for about 2–3 minutes on each side for medium-rare or until cooked to your liking. Remove from the pan and allow to cool slightly.

Arrange the lettuce in the middle of each of four serving plates and drizzle lightly with the remaining oil. Break each salmon fillet into four pieces and arrange over the lettuce. Sprinkle the watercress on top, drizzle with the dressing, and serve at once.

Serves 4

pepper-crusted salmon salad

eggplant and lentil salad

3 tablespoons olive oil
1/2 large eggplant (about
    11 oz.), cut into
      1/4-inch cubes
1 small red onion, finely diced
1/4 teaspoon ground cumin
3 garlic cloves, chopped

1 cup French green lentils
    or green lentils
1 1/2 cups vegetable stock
2 tablespoons chopped parsley
1 tablespoon red wine vinegar
1 tablespoon extra-virgin
    olive oil

Heat 2 tablespoons of the olive oil in a large frying pan. Add the eggplant and cook over medium heat, stirring constantly, for 5 minutes or until soft. Add the onion and cumin and sauté for 2–3 minutes or until the onion has softened. Transfer to a serving bowl and season well.

Heat the remaining olive oil in the frying pan. Add the garlic and cook over medium heat for 1 minute, then add the lentils and stock and cook, stirring regularly, over low heat for 30–40 minutes or until the liquid has evaporated and the lentils are tender.

Add the lentils to the eggplant and stir in the parsley and vinegar. Season well, drizzle with the extra-virgin olive oil, and serve.

Serves 4

red potato salad with dill and mustard dressing

6 red potatoes (about 2 1/2 lb.)

dill and mustard dressing
1 tablespoon seeded mustard
1 1/2 tablespoons chopped dill

2 teaspoons brown sugar
3 tablespoons red wine vinegar
4 tablespoons olive oil

Bring a large pot of lightly salted water to a boil. Add the potatoes and cook for 20 minutes or until tender. Drain well and allow to cool slightly.

Meanwhile, make the dill and mustard dressing. Mix the mustard, dill, sugar, and vinegar together in a small bowl, then whisk in the oil until well combined.

When the potatoes are cool enough to handle, cut them into 1-inch chunks. Gently toss the dressing through the warm potatoes, season to taste, and serve warm.

Serves 4

On an icy winter's evening, stoke the home fires, open a bottle of your favorite red, and tuck into a bowl of this fulsome dish.

warm roasted potato with spicy sausage

6 small waxy potatoes, unpeeled
2 tablespoons olive oil
1 teaspoon sea salt
4 small chorizo sausages (about 1 lb.), cut into 1/2-inch slices
1 small bunch arugula, leaves trimmed and roughly torn
3/4 cup sun-dried tomatoes
crusty bread, to serve

whole-grain mustard dressing
3 tablespoons olive oil
1 tablespoon whole-grain mustard
2 tablespoons sherry vinegar or white wine vinegar

Preheat the oven to 400°F. Scrub the potatoes and pat them dry. Put them in a roasting pan without any oil or seasoning and bake for 20 minutes or until starting to soften. Remove from the oven and gently squash each potato using a potato masher, until the skins burst and they are slightly flattened. Lightly drizzle the oil over each potato, sprinkle with the sea salt, and gently toss to coat. Roast for an additional 10–15 minutes or until crispy and golden.

Meanwhile, put a frying pan over high heat. Add the chorizo and dry-fry for about 5 minutes or until cooked through and golden. Transfer to a serving dish with the arugula and tomatoes.

Put all the whole-grain mustard dressing ingredients in a small bowl. Whisk well and season lightly with salt and freshly ground black pepper.

Add the crispy potatoes to the salad, pour the dressing over, and toss well. Serve hot or warm, with crusty bread.

Serves 4

warm roasted potato with spicy sausage

warm shrimp, arugula, and feta salad

3 scallions

3 plum tomatoes

1 small red bell pepper

15-oz. can chickpeas, rinsed
and drained

1/2 tablespoon chopped dill

2 tablespoons finely
shredded basil

2 tablespoons olive oil

3 tablespoons butter

1 1/2 lb. raw shrimp, peeled and
deveined, tails intact

1 small red chili, finely chopped

3 garlic cloves, crushed

1 1/2 tablespoons lemon juice

2 small bunches arugula,
trimmed

4 oz. feta cheese, crumbled

Chop the scallions, tomatoes, and bell pepper and place in a bowl with the chickpeas, dill, and basil. Toss well.

Heat the oil and butter in a large frying pan. Add the shrimp and cook, stirring, over high heat for 2 minutes. Add the chili and garlic and continue cooking until the shrimp turn pink. Remove from the heat and stir in the lemon juice.

Arrange the arugula on a large platter and top with the tomato mixture, then the shrimp mixture. Sprinkle with the crumbled feta and serve.

Serves 4

mini meatballs with couscous and yogurt

1 1/4 lb. lean ground beef
1 teaspoon chili flakes
1 teaspoon ground cumin
2 tablespoons chopped pitted
   black olives
1 small onion, grated
2 tablespoons tomato paste
3–4 tablespoons olive oil

1 1/2 cups instant couscous
9-oz. carton cherry tomatoes,
   halved
1/2 cup roasted red bell pepper,
   diced
3/4 cup plain yogurt
2 tablespoons lemon juice
2 tablespoons chopped parsley

Put the beef, chili flakes, cumin, olives, onion, and tomato paste in a bowl. Season, mix well with your hands, and roll into forty balls. Chill for 30 minutes.

Put 1 1/4 cups water in a saucepan with 2 tablespoons of the oil and 2 teaspoons of salt. Bring to a boil, remove from the heat, and add the couscous. Stir, then cover and let stand for 2–3 minutes. Fluff up with a fork and add the tomatoes and bell pepper. Season and mix well.

Heat the remaining oil in a large frying pan. Fry the meatballs over medium heat for 10–12 minutes or until cooked through, then arrange them over the couscous. Mix the yogurt, lemon juice, and parsley together with 1 tablespoon water, drizzle over the meatballs, and serve.

Serves 4

The sweet chili marinade tenderizes the octopus, gently coaxing it into yielding a wealth of soft, spicy secrets.

Thai marinated octopus salad

8 baby octopus, or 4 large
   octopus cut in half
   (about 13 oz. in total)
1 cup sweet chili sauce
2 tablespoons lime juice

1 stem lemongrass, white part
   only, finely chopped
2 cucumbers
4 butter lettuce leaves, torn
4 large handfuls cilantro,
   with stalks

Using a small, sharp knife, carefully cut between the head and tentacles of the octopus, just below the eyes. Grasp the body of the octopus and push the beak out and up through the center of the tentacles with your finger. Cut the eyes from the head of the octopus by slicing off a small disk and discard the eye section. To clean the octopus head, carefully slit through one side, avoiding the ink sac, and scrape out any gut from inside. Rinse under running water to remove any remaining gut.

Put the octopuses in a nonmetallic bowl and add the sweet chili sauce, lime juice, and lemongrass. Stir until well mixed and thoroughly coated. Cover with plastic wrap and marinate for 4 hours.

Cut the cucumbers into 2$\frac{1}{2}$-inch lengths, scoop out the seeds, and then julienne the flesh. Arrange the lettuce and cilantro around the edge of a large serving plate.

Heat a frying pan or charbroil pan to high. Remove the octopuses from the marinade, reserving the marinade, and then fry them for about 3–4 minutes or until tender and cooked through. Remove and pile in the middle of the serving plate.

Add the reserved marinade to the pan and heat through for 2 minutes. Stir the cucumber into the marinade to warm through, then spoon the marinade all over the salad and serve at once.

Serves 4

mini meatballs with couscous and yogurt

squash and shrimp salad with arugula

1/2 butternut squash, peeled and cut into 1¼-inch cubes

2 small red onions, cut into thick wedges

1 tablespoon vegetable oil

2 cloves garlic, crushed

11 oz. cooked shrimp, peeled and deveined

1¾ cups baby arugula leaves

1–2 tablespoons balsamic vinegar

1 tablespoon olive oil

Preheat the oven to 400°F. Toss the squash and onions in a large bowl with the oil and garlic. Spread in a single layer on a baking sheet and bake for 25–30 minutes or until tender. Transfer to a serving bowl, add the shrimp and arugula, and gently toss together.

Whisk together the vinegar and oil and season to taste with sea salt and freshly ground black pepper. Drizzle over the salad and serve.

Serves 4

mussel salad with warm saffron dressing

1 lb. new potatoes
2¹/₄ lb. black mussels
²/₃ cup dry white wine
1 small onion, sliced
2 thyme sprigs

2 fresh or dried bay leaves
large pinch of powdered saffron
4 tablespoons sour cream
2 teaspoons chopped parsley

Cook the potatoes in salted boiling water until tender. Drain and allow to cool slightly. Meanwhile, scrub the mussels with a stiff brush and pull out the hairy beards. Discard any broken mussels or open ones that don't close when tapped on the counter. Rinse well under running water.

Put the wine, onion, thyme, bay leaves, and half the mussels in a pot. Cover and cook over high heat, stirring once, for 3–4 minutes or until the mussels start to open. Remove the mussels as they open and discard any unopened ones. Cook the remaining mussels and allow to cool slightly. Strain the mussel stock, reserving 1/2 cup. While the liquid is still warm, stir in the saffron. Whisk in the sour cream and season well.

Quarter any large potatoes and halve the small ones. Remove the mussels from their shells, place in a serving bowl with the potatoes, and gently mix in the warm saffron dressing. Sprinkle with the parsley and serve.

Serves 4

Lovely lamb gets an extra lift from the herbal scent of fresh mint and a burst of tiny sweet tomatoes.

minted lamb salad with haloumi

2 tablespoons olive oil
1 lb. lamb tenderloin, trimmed
1 head red-leaf lettuce, leaves
   torn
8 yellow pear tomatoes
8 cherry tomatoes
4 oz. haloumi cheese, cut into
   $1/2$ x $1^1/2$-inch fingers

mint and mustard dressing
3 tablespoons olive oil
1 tablespoon white wine
   vinegar
$1/2$ teaspoon French mustard
1 tablespoon chopped mint
$1/2$ teaspoon sugar

Heat half the oil in a heavy-based pan over medium-high heat. Add the lamb tenderloin and cook, turning frequently, for 7–8 minutes for medium-rare (do not overcook the lamb—it should still be pink in the middle). Transfer to a plate, cover loosely with foil, and allow to stand for 5–10 minutes. Thinly slice the lamb diagonally.

Divide the lettuce between four serving plates and arrange the tomatoes and lamb slices over the top.

Put all the mint and mustard dressing ingredients in a small screw-top jar, then shake well and set aside.

Heat the remaining oil in the pan. Add the haloumi and cook over medium heat for 2 minutes or until golden, turning occasionally. Drain on crumpled paper towels and arrange on top of the salad. Briefly shake the dressing again, drizzle over the salad, and serve immediately.

Serves 4

squash and shrimp salad with arugula

mushroom and shredded chicken salad

1–2 tablespoons olive oil
2 cups small button mushrooms
2 cups other mixed mushrooms
    (such as brown cremini and
    shiitake), larger ones halved
    or quartered
4 cups cooked chicken, shredded
4 cups mixed salad leaves

lime and soy dressing

2 tablespoons lime juice
1 tablespoon soy sauce
2 tablespoons olive oil
1 tablespoon sweet chili sauce
1 tablespoon red wine vinegar

Heat 1 tablespoon of the oil in a frying pan. Add the mushrooms and cook over medium heat for 2–3 minutes or until softened. Toss in a large bowl with the shredded chicken.

Combine all the lime and soy dressing ingredients in a small bowl, mix well, and pour two thirds over the warm mushrooms.

Arrange the salad leaves in a serving dish and toss through the remaining dressing. Top with the chicken and mushrooms and serve warm.

Serves 4

warm chicken and pasta salad

5 cups penne
1/2 cup olive oil
4 slender eggplants, thinly sliced
    diagonally
2 boneless, skinless chicken
    breasts
2 teaspoons lemon juice

2 handfuls parsley, chopped
1 1/2 cups charbroiled red bell
    pepper slices
1 bunch asparagus spears,
    trimmed and blanched
1/2 cup sun-dried tomatoes, sliced
grated Parmesan cheese, to serve

Cook the pasta in a large pot of boiling salted water until al dente. Drain, return to the pan, and keep warm.

Meanwhile, heat 2 tablespoons of the oil in a large frying pan. Fry the eggplant over high heat for 4–5 minutes or until golden and cooked through; remove. Heat another 2 tablespoons of oil in the pan, reduce the heat to medium, and cook the chicken for 4–5 minutes on each side or until lightly browned and cooked through. Allow to cool, then thickly slice.

Put the remaining oil in a small screw-top jar with the lemon juice and parsley and shake well. Return the pasta to the heat and mix in the dressing, chicken, eggplant, bell pepper, asparagus, and tomatoes to warm through. Season with black pepper, sprinkle with Parmesan, and serve.

Serves 4

The mellow warmth of roast garlic and the sharp tang of feta balance the sweetness of the beet and sweet potato.

roasted beet and sweet potato salad with feta

6 baby beets, trimmed
and scrubbed
1 orange sweet potato, peeled
and cut into 3/4-inch chunks
3 tablespoons garlic oil (see Note)
1 garlic bulb
1 1/2 tablespoons butter
3 tablespoons olive oil

1 red onion, cut into wedges
1 tablespoon balsamic vinegar
1 teaspoon brown sugar
1 1/2 cups baby spinach leaves
2 rosemary sprigs
2 tablespoons lemon juice
1 tablespoon shredded basil
4 oz. feta cheese

Preheat the oven to 350°F. Arrange the beets on a baking sheet. Brush the sweet potato with the garlic oil and season; place on another baking sheet with the whole garlic bulb. Roast the vegetables for 35–40 minutes or until tender when pierced with a knife. Remove from the oven and allow to cool, then peel the beets, wearing gloves.

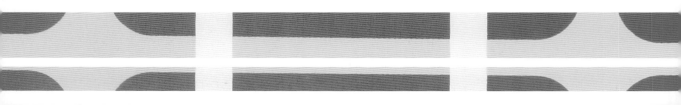

Heat the butter and 1 tablespoon of the olive oil in a small saucepan. When the butter has melted, add the onion and cook over medium heat, stirring occasionally, for 15 minutes or until soft. Add the vinegar and sugar and cook for 3–5 minutes or until the onion is golden and starting to caramelize. Place in a serving bowl with the roasted beet, sweet potato, spinach, and rosemary leaves and mix together gently.

Slip the roasted garlic cloves from their skins into a small bowl. Add the remaining olive oil, lemon juice, and basil and whisk together well to make a dressing, then season to taste. Crumble the feta over the salad, drizzle with the roasted garlic dressing, and serve.

Note: If you are unable to obtain garlic oil, you can make your own by steeping some crushed garlic in extra-virgin olive oil for 2 hours, then straining it. Alternatively, use plain olive oil for this recipe.

Serves 4

mushroom and shredded chicken salad

calamari and scallops with chermoula dressing

8 baby calamari, cleaned and
    rinsed
7 oz. scallops, without roe
2 tablespoons vegetable oil
1 bunch arugula, trimmed
3 ripe plum tomatoes, chopped
2 oranges, peeled and
    segmented

chermoula dressing
4 large handfuls cilantro, finely
    chopped
2 large handfuls Italian parsley,
    chopped
2 teaspoons ground cumin
1 teaspoon ground paprika
3 tablespoons lime juice
3 tablespoons olive oil

Put the calamari in a bowl of water with 1/4 teaspoon salt. Mix well, then chill for 30 minutes. Drain well, then cut the tubes into long thin strips and the tentacles into pieces. Rinse the scallops and pat them dry with paper towels.

Heat the oil in a large, deep frying pan. Cook the calamari in batches over high heat for 1 minute or until they turn white. Remove and drain. Fry the scallops in small batches over high heat for 1 minute on each side, until golden.

Arrange the arugula on a large platter and top with the seafood, tomatoes, and orange segments. Quickly whisk the chermoula dressing ingredients together in a nonmetallic bowl, pour over the seafood, and serve.

Serves 4

warm pasta and crab salad

11 oz. thin spaghetti

2 tablespoons olive oil

1¹/₂ tablespoons butter, chopped

12 oz. fresh crabmeat

1 red bell pepper, cut into thin strips

1¹/₂ teaspoons finely grated lemon zest

3 tablespoons grated Parmesan cheese

2 tablespoons snipped chives

3 tablespoons chopped parsley

Break all the spaghetti in half and cook in a large pot of boiling salted water until al dente. Drain well, then place in a large serving bowl and toss with the oil and butter.

Add the crabmeat, bell pepper, lemon zest, Parmesan, chives, and parsley, and toss to combine. Sprinkle with freshly ground black pepper and serve.

Serves 4

Italian-style chicken and pasta salad

14 oz. boneless, skinless
 chicken breasts
3 tablespoons lemon juice
2 small garlic cloves, crushed
1 tablespoon seasoned lemon
 pepper
1½ tablespoons olive oil
3⅓ cups penne, cooked
4 oz. prosciutto, sliced into
 thin strips
1 cucumber, cut in half
 lengthwise, then sliced
⅓ cup thinly sliced sun-dried
 tomatoes

⅓ cup pitted black olives,
 halved
4 bottled artichoke hearts,
 halved
¼ cup shaved Parmesan cheese

creamy basil sauce

3 tablespoons olive oil
1 tablespoon white wine
 vinegar
1 teaspoon Dijon mustard
1 tablespoon cornstarch
⅔ cup cream
4 tablespoons shredded basil

Flatten the chicken breasts slightly with a mallet or rolling pin. Mix the lemon juice and garlic in a bowl, add the chicken fillets, and turn until coated all over. Cover with plastic wrap and refrigerate for at least 3 hours or overnight, turning occasionally.

Drain the chicken and coat in the seasoned lemon pepper. Heat the oil in a large, heavy-based frying pan. Add the chicken and cook over medium heat for 4–5 minutes on each side or until lightly browned and cooked through. Remove from the heat, allow to cool, then cut into thin slices.

To make the creamy basil sauce, combine the oil, vinegar, and mustard in a saucepan with a little salt and freshly ground pepper. Blend the cornstarch with 4 tablespoons of water in a small bowl until smooth. Add to the pan and whisk over medium heat for 2 minutes or until the sauce boils and thickens. Add the cream and basil, adjust the seasoning, and stir until heated through.

Combine the pasta, chicken, prosciutto, cucumber, tomatoes, olives, and artichokes in a large serving bowl. Pour over the warm sauce and toss gently to combine. Sprinkle with the shaved Parmesan and serve.

Serves 4

warm pasta and crab salad

eggplant salad

10 slender eggplants
2 tablespoons peanut oil
3 red Asian shallots, finely sliced
2 garlic cloves, crushed
1 red chili, finely chopped
1 hard-boiled egg, peeled
    and diced
1 tablespoon crisp fried red Asian
    shallot flakes
2 tablespoons cilantro leaves

dressing
1 teaspoon brown sugar
2 tablespoons soy sauce
1–2 teaspoons fish sauce
2 tablespoons lime juice
1 tablespoon toasted
    sesame seeds

Preheat the oven to 400°F. Put the eggplants in a roasting pan with half the oil and toss to coat. Bake for 15 minutes or until tender. Remove from the oven and allow to cool, then peel away the skin and cut the flesh into 3/4-inch chunks.

Heat the remaining oil in a frying pan. Add the shallots, garlic, and chili and cook over medium heat for 2 minutes or until soft. Transfer to a mortar and pestle and pound into a paste, then mix with the eggplant.

Put the dressing ingredients in a bowl and stir until the sugar has dissolved. Spoon the eggplant mixture onto a serving platter and top with the egg, shallot flakes, and cilantro. Pour the dressing over and serve at once.

Serves 4

roasted fennel, beet, and smoked trout salad

12 baby beets
2–3 tablespoons olive oil
2 large fennel bulbs (about
    7 oz. each)
4 oz. smoked trout fillet,
    broken into chunks
crusty bread, to serve

horseradish dressing
$2/3$ cup sour cream
1 tablespoon creamed
    horseradish
1 tablespoon lemon juice
2 tablespoons snipped chives

Preheat the oven to 400°F. Wearing gloves, peel the beets, then cut the bulbs into chunks. Place in a large roasting pan and drizzle with 2 tablespoons of the oil. Season with salt and pepper and toss to coat, then cover with foil and roast for 40–45 minutes or until tender.

Meanwhile, cut off and discard the stalks and fronds from the fennel. Cut the bulbs into quarters and blanch in boiling salted water for 5 minutes or until tender. Drain well and cut into smaller wedges. Add to the beet for the final 30 minutes of cooking, adding a little extra oil if needed.

Put the beet and fennel in a serving dish with the smoked trout. Combine the horseradish dressing ingredients in a small bowl and dollop over the salad. Serve warm with crusty bread.

Serves 4

Roasting tomatoes intensifies their sweetness and reveals a depth of flavor that exquisitely complements the seared lamb.

lamb with roasted tomatoes

6 vine-ripened tomatoes
4 garlic cloves, finely chopped
1 tablespoon chopped oregano
1 tablespoon chopped parsley
3 tablespoons olive oil
3 bunches asparagus spears, trimmed
2 lamb tenderloins (1 lb. total)

mint yogurt dressing
1 tablespoon red wine vinegar
$1/2$ cucumber, finely diced
$1/3$ cup thick plain yogurt
2 teaspoons chopped mint
$1/2$ teaspoon ground cumin
1 tablespoon olive oil

Preheat the oven to 350°F. Cut the tomatoes in half and scoop out the seeds. In a small bowl, mix together the garlic, oregano, and parsley, then sprinkle the mixture into the tomato shells. Put the tomatoes on a rack in a roasting pan, drizzle with 1 tablespoon of the oil, and roast for 1 hour. Remove the tomato halves from the oven, again cut them into halves, and keep warm.

Put the asparagus in the roasting pan and drizzle with another tablespoon of the oil. Season and roast for 10 minutes.

Meanwhile, heat the remaining oil in a frying pan. Season the lamb well and cook over medium-high heat for 5 minutes on each side, then remove from the heat, cover with foil, and let stand for 5–10 minutes.

Put all the mint yogurt dressing ingredients in a small bowl and whisk together well. Arrange the asparagus on a serving platter and top with the roasted tomatoes. Slice the lamb diagonally and arrange on top of the tomatoes. Drizzle with the dressing and serve immediately.

Serves 4

roasted fennel, beet, and smoked trout salad

ground pork and noodle salad

1 tablespoon peanut oil
1 lb. ground pork
2 garlic cloves, finely chopped
1 stem lemongrass, white
    part only, finely chopped
3 red Asian shallots, finely sliced
1 tablespoon finely grated
    fresh ginger
1 small red chili, finely chopped
5 kaffir lime leaves, very
    finely shredded
6 oz. glass (mung bean) noodles
1/2 cup baby spinach leaves

4 large handfuls cilantro,
    chopped
1 large handful mint leaves

dressing

1 1/2 tablespoons brown sugar
2 tablespoons fish sauce
4 tablespoons lime juice
2 teaspoons sesame oil
2 teaspoons peanut oil

Heat a wok until very hot, add the oil, and swirl to coat. Stir-fry the pork in batches over high heat for 5 minutes or until golden. Add the garlic, lemongrass, shallots, ginger, chili, and lime leaves and stir-fry until fragrant.

Cover the noodles with boiling water to soften. Rinse, drain, and toss in a bowl with the pork, spinach, cilantro, and mint. Whisk together the dressing ingredients and toss through the salad. Season with pepper and serve.

Serves 4

roasted vegetables with pan-fried garlic bread crumbs

3 zucchini, sliced
2¹/₂ cups button mushrooms,
    larger ones halved
1 red onion, cut into 8 wedges
1 red bell pepper, diced
3 tablespoons olive oil
1 garlic clove, crushed

¹/₂ cup bread crumbs, made
    from day-old bread

dressing
1 tablespoon olive oil
2 tablespoons store-bought pesto
1 tablespoon lemon juice

Preheat the oven to 400°F. Put all the vegetables in a large baking dish. Drizzle with 2 tablespoons of the oil, add a little salt and pepper, and shake the pan to coat all the vegetables in the oil. Roast for 30 minutes or until all the vegetables are tender.

Combine the dressing ingredients in a large serving bowl. Add the roasted vegetables, toss gently, and let stand for 10 minutes for the flavors to mingle.

Heat the remaining oil in a frying pan and fry the garlic over medium heat for about 30 seconds. Increase the heat, add the bread crumbs, and fry for 2–3 minutes or until golden, shaking the pan and stirring the crumbs. Toss the toasted bread crumbs through the salad and serve.

Serves 4

Seriously spicy and fabulously fragrant, this tortilla-topped salad offers a healthy taste of Mexico without the heft.

blackened chicken with crispy tortillas

4 vine-ripened tomatoes, cut into $1/2$-inch slices
1 teaspoon superfine sugar
1 red onion, sliced
$2/3$ cup olive oil
1 teaspoon ground oregano
$2^1/2$ teaspoons ground cumin
$1^1/4$ teaspoons garlic salt
$1/2$ teaspoon cayenne pepper
4 small boneless, skinless chicken breasts

2 corn tortillas, each 6 inches round, cut into $3/4$-inch strips
2 handfuls cilantro leaves

guacamole dressing
1 ripe avocado
$1/4$ cup sour cream
$1/3$ cup milk
2 tablespoons lime juice

Arrange the tomato slices in a wide dish, sprinkle with the sugar, and season well. Layer the onion on top and drizzle with 3 tablespoons of the oil. Cover and refrigerate for 20 minutes.

To make the guacamole dressing, blend the avocado, sour cream, milk, and lime juice in a food processor with 4 tablespoons of water for about 1 minute or until smooth. Season.

Combine the oregano, cumin, garlic salt, and cayenne pepper in a small bowl and use it to coat the chicken breasts, pressing down firmly with your fingers. Heat 1$^1/_2$ tablespoons of oil over medium heat in a large nonstick frying pan until hot. Cook the chicken breasts for 4–5 minutes on each side or until cooked through. Remove and allow to cool a little.

In the same pan, heat the remaining oil. Fry the tortilla strips until golden, turning once during cooking.

Arrange the tomato and onion slices in a circle on four serving plates. Slice each chicken breast diagonally into $^3/_4$-inch strips and place on top of the tomato. Spoon the dressing over and top with the tortilla strips. Sprinkle with the cilantro and serve hot.

Serves 4

roasted vegetables with pan-fried garlic bread crumbs

warm mixed bean salad

2 tablespoons olive oil
1/2 cup tomato juice
2 tablespoons chopped
   Italian parsley
pinch of sugar
3 garlic cloves

15-oz. can cranberry beans,
   drained and rinsed
15-oz. can cannellini beans,
   drained and rinsed
2 tomatoes, diced
4 thick slices crusty bread

Put 1 tablespoon of the oil in a small bowl with the tomato juice, parsley, and sugar. Crush two of the garlic cloves and stir them into the mixture.

Put the cranberry and cannellini beans in a frying pan, add the tomato juice mixture, and warm over medium heat for about 5 minutes or until well warmed through. Mix in the diced tomatoes and season to taste.

Meanwhile, toast the bread slices. Cut the remaining garlic clove and rub the cut side all over the bread. Drizzle with the remaining oil and serve hot with the warm beans.

Serves 4

warm lentil and rice salad

3/4 cup olive oil

2 tablespoons butter

3 large red onions, finely sliced

3 garlic cloves, crushed

2 teaspoons ground cinnamon

2 teaspoons ground sweet
   paprika

2 teaspoons ground cumin

2 teaspoons ground coriander

3/4 cup green lentils

3/4 cup basmati rice

3 scallions, finely chopped

Heat the oil and butter in a frying pan. When the butter has melted, add the onion and garlic and cook over low heat, stirring, for 30 minutes or until very soft. Stir in the ground cinnamon, paprika, cumin, and coriander and cook for a few minutes longer, until aromatic. Keep warm.

Meanwhile, bring a pot of water to a boil, add the rice, and cook until the grains are just tender. While the rice is cooking, bring another pot of water to a boil, add the lentils, and cook until just tender.

Drain the rice and lentils well, then transfer to a large serving bowl and mix in the onion mixture, scallions, and freshly ground black pepper to taste. Serve warm.

Serves 4

Pancetta, sage, and parsley bring Continental chutzpah to this sophisticated salad, with a splash of sherry to help make merry.

fusilli salad with sherry vinaigrette

2 cups fusilli or other spiral pasta
1 1/3 cups small cauliflower florets
1/2 cup toasted pine nuts
4 tablespoons olive oil
10 slices pancetta
1 small handful small sage leaves
1 1/2 tablespoons finely chopped red Asian shallots
1 tablespoon sherry vinegar
1 small red chili, finely chopped
2 garlic cloves, crushed
1 teaspoon brown sugar
2 tablespoons orange juice
1 large handful parsley, finely chopped
1/4 cup shaved Parmesan cheese

Cook the pasta in a large pot of boiling salted water until al dente. Drain, rinse under cold water, and drain again.

Blanch the cauliflower florets in boiling water for 2–3 minutes, then drain and cool. Place in a large serving bowl with the pasta and pine nuts.

Heat 1 tablespoon of the oil in a nonstick frying pan and cook the pancetta for 2 minutes or until crisp. Remove and drain on crumpled paper towels. Add 1 more tablespoon of oil and fry the sage leaves for 1 minute or until crisp. Remove and drain on crumpled paper towels.

Heat the remaining oil in the pan, add the shallots, and cook gently for 2 minutes or until soft. Remove from the heat, then stir in the vinegar, chili, garlic, sugar, orange juice, and parsley. Pour the warm dressing over the pasta and toss gently. Crumble the pancetta on top and sprinkle with the sage leaves and shaved Parmesan. Serve warm.

Serves 4

warm mixed bean salad

warm Thai tuna salad

1¹/2 lb. fresh tuna steaks
1 tablespoon olive oil
2 tablespoons oyster sauce
2 tablespoons soy sauce
2 tablespoons lime juice
10 oz. dried egg noodles
2/3 cup baby corn, halved
1¹/2 cups snow peas, trimmed

cilantro chili dressing
2 tablespoons fish sauce
2 tablespoons lime juice
2 tablespoons Thai sweet
  chili sauce
2 tablespoons vegetable oil
1 small red chili, chopped
3 tablespoons chopped cilantro

Put the tuna in a shallow dish in a single layer. Whisk together the oil, oyster sauce, soy sauce, and lime juice and pour the mixture over the tuna, turning to coat all over. Cover and refrigerate for 30 minutes.

Cook the noodles according to the package instructions, adding the corn and snow peas for the final 45 seconds. Drain well, then toss in a serving bowl. Combine the dressing ingredients and mix half through the noodles.

Heat a charbroil pan to high. Cook the tuna for 3–4 minutes on each side, so it's still pink in the middle. Cool slightly, then slice into strips. Serve separately or over the noodles, with the remaining dressing on the side.

Serves 4

salmon and green bean salad

2 teaspoons olive oil
10 oz. skinless salmon fillet
vegetable oil, for deep-frying
3 garlic cloves, thinly sliced
1 white sweet potato,
    thinly sliced
2/3 cup green beans, trimmed
    and blanched
1 small red onion, thinly sliced
1 tablespoon toasted sesame
    seeds

1 head mizuna lettuce, leaves
    torn

lime and tahini dressing
2 garlic cloves, crushed
1 1/2 tablespoons tahini
1 tablespoon rice vinegar
1 1/2 tablespoons lime juice
1 tablespoon soy sauce
2 tablespoons olive oil

Heat the oil in a frying pan. Cook the salmon over medium heat for 2–3 minutes on each side. Cool slightly, then cut into chunks.

Fill a deep-fryer or wok one-third full of oil and heat to 350°F or until a cube of bread dropped in the oil browns in 15 seconds. In separate batches, cook the garlic and sweet potato until golden and crisp, then drain.

Whisk together the dressing ingredients. Toss the garlic and sweet potato in a bowl with the beans, onion, sesame seeds, and lettuce. Divide among four serving plates, top with salmon, drizzle with the dressing, and serve.

Serves 4

Baby spinach makes a delicate bed for the chicken, with a refreshing dressing of garlic, mint, and cider vinegar.

warm minted chicken and pasta salad

3 cups fusilli or other spiral pasta
1/2 cup olive oil
1 large red bell pepper
3 boneless, skinless chicken breasts
6 scallions, cut into 3/4-inch lengths
4 garlic cloves, thinly sliced
4 tablespoons cider vinegar
3 large handfuls mint leaves, chopped
2 cups baby spinach leaves

Cook the pasta in a large pot of boiling salted water until al dente. Drain, transfer to a large serving bowl, and stir in 1 tablespoon of the oil.

Meanwhile, cut the bell pepper into large flat pieces and remove the seeds and membranes. Cook, skin side up, under a hot broiler for

8–10 minutes or until the skin blackens and blisters. Allow to cool in a plastic bag, then peel away the skin and cut the bell pepper into thin strips.

Place the chicken between two sheets of plastic wrap and press with the palm of your hand until slightly flattened.

Heat 1 tablespoon of the oil in a large frying pan. Add the chicken and cook over medium heat for 4–5 minutes on each side or until lightly browned and cooked through. Remove from the pan and allow to cool a little. Cut into thin slices and add to the pasta.

Heat another tablespoon of the oil in the pan. Add the scallions, garlic, and roasted bell pepper and cook, stirring, for 2–3 minutes or until starting to soften. Add the remaining oil, vinegar, and most of the mint leaves and stir until warmed through. Add to the pasta with the spinach and remaining mint, toss well, and season to taste. Serve warm.

Serves 4

warm Thai tuna salad

warm choy sum salad

1 bunch choy sum (Chinese
   flowering cabbage)
2 tablespoons peanut oil
1 tablespoon finely grated
   fresh ginger
2 garlic cloves, finely chopped

2 teaspoons sugar
2 teaspoons sesame oil
2 tablespoons soy sauce
1 tablespoon lemon juice
2 teaspoons toasted sesame
   seeds

Trim the ends from the choy sum and slice the leaves in half. Steam for about 2 minutes or until just wilted.

Heat a small saucepan to very hot, add the peanut oil, and swirl to coat the pan. Add the ginger and garlic and stir-fry for 1 minute. Add the sugar, sesame oil, soy sauce, and lemon juice and heat until hot.

Arrange the choy sum on a serving plate and pour over the hot dressing. Season to taste, sprinkle with the sesame seeds, and serve.

Serves 4

warm pork salad with blue cheese toasts

1/2 cup olive oil
1 large garlic clove, crushed
14 oz. pork tenderloin, cut
    into 1/4-inch slices
1 small or 1/2 a large French
    baguette

4 oz. blue cheese, crumbled
2 tablespoons sherry vinegar
1/2 teaspoon brown sugar
3 cups mixed salad leaves

Put the oil and garlic in a screw-top jar and shake well. Heat 2 teaspoons of the garlic oil mixture in a frying pan over medium-high heat. Add half the pork slices and cook for 1 minute on each side, then remove and keep warm. Add another 2 teaspoons of the garlic oil and cook the remaining pork. Remove, keep warm, and season all the pork with salt and pepper.

Cut the bread into twenty thin slices and spread on a baking sheet. Brush the tops with a little garlic oil and cook under a hot broiler until golden, about 1–2 minutes. Turn the bread over, sprinkle with the blue cheese, then broil for about 30 seconds to melt the cheese.

Add the vinegar and sugar to the remaining garlic oil and shake well. Put the salad leaves in a large bowl, add the pork, and pour on the salad dressing. Toss well. Place a mound of salad in the middle of each of four serving plates and arrange five toasts around the edge of each. Serve at once.

Serves 4

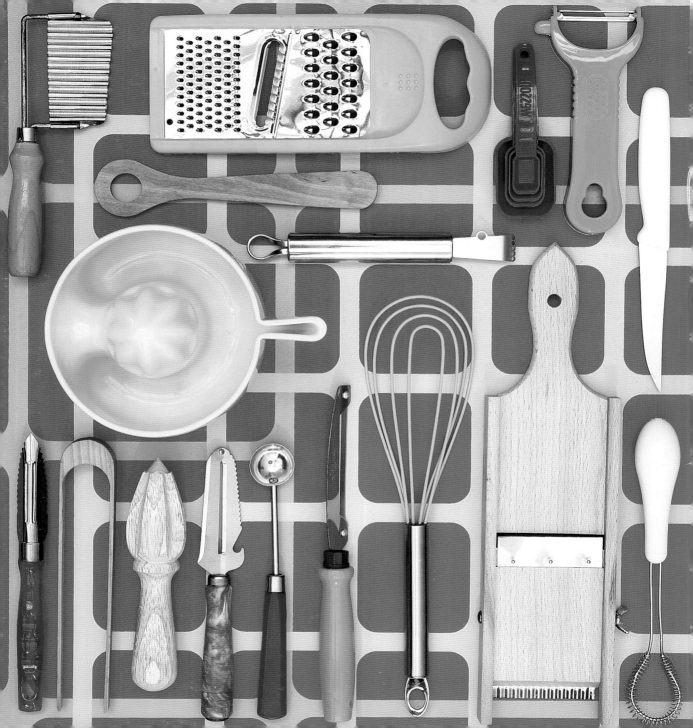

index

427

429